40 Something

My warmest thanks to you for buying my book. You are personally invited to join the 40 Something Community and be among the first to know of my latest content, workshops, and retreats curated especially for you. Join us here:

www.40somethingthemovement.com/book

I'd love to have you!

40 Something

10 Radical Lessons for Women on How to Live and Love Without Losing Themselves

Darnise C. Martin, PhD

CHYVONNE PUBLISHING
Los Angeles

40 Something: 10 Radical Lessons for Women on How to Live and Love Without Losing Themselves
Published by Chyvonne Publishing, Los Angeles

Copyright © 2019 by Darnise C. Martin

All rights reserved. Aside from brief passages in a published review, no part of this book may be reproduced or transmitted in any form or by any means, electronic or mechanical, including all technologies known or later developed, without written permission from the publisher.

Paperback ISBN: 978-0-578-49778-5

Cover designer: Brad Norr
Publishing consultant: Beth Wright, Wright for Writers LLC

Contents

Introduction ~ 1

The 10 Radical Lessons

1. Be Open to Growth ~ 5
2. Heal Your Childhood Wounds ~ 16
3. Face Your Fears ~ 26
4. Identify Your Values and Priorities ~ 43
5. Be Authentic in All Aspects of Your Life ~ 53
6. Learn from the Patterns in Your Life ~ 69
7. Set Healthy Boundaries ~ 78
8. Rely on Your Faith ~ 90
9. Take Time for Self-Care ~ 99
10. Remember That You Are Enough ~ 108

Conclusion ~ 114

Afterword ~ 116

Acknowledgments ~ 118

Introduction

***40 Something* has** been a labor of love for me.

At first I didn't know if I should write this book, at least not in this way. It's personal and intimate, and I'm not the kind of person to make private things public. However, I'm good at helping other people through their struggles and revelations, so I felt compelled to use the intimate details of my own life to help other women find their way. Once I began writing, I knew that I would have to be transparent. I would have to be honest and authentic about my struggles because they are what brought me to my revelations and epiphanies. They are what make me an effective, empathetic coach and mentor to others.

I wrote this book for women who are revisiting themselves. I wrote it for women who've consistently given so much over the years, and who now stop to ask, Have I given so much that I don't have anything left for myself? I wrote for the woman who is feeling a void in her life because she doesn't know where she fits in anymore. Her roles have shifted, and finally she is taking time for herself, reviewing her goals and her dreams in light of all the peaks and valleys that she's encountered on her life's journey. She has struggled at times but senses that now at forty-something she is called to be front and center in her own life. I wrote for this woman who is ready to stand in the wisdom that her past has taught her, take a deep breath, and craft new pathways for herself.

She may have felt her setbacks or so-called failings meant that she was less than. She may have never shared with anyone how many times she doubted herself or cried alone. She may have sabotaged herself by dimming her own light and playing small. Maybe she chose the wrong partner and ended up feeling heartbroken and stupid for falling for the same thing again.

I wrote this book so that women could look back at their personal experiences and draw strength, clarity, confidence, and courage. I want each woman who reads it to be able to own who she has been, learn and adjust as necessary, and create a life exactly how she wants it to be. I want her to see through my experiences that when things go wrong, it's not because something is wrong with her. I want her to know how normal it is to have challenges and to fail and get back up again. I want her to know that no matter what her role is for others—wife, mother, sister, daughter, best friend, employee, business owner—she must first of all be true to herself and find sustenance for her own soul. I want her to know that her life experiences have positioned her for this moment, and that she can recreate herself just as she wants to be.

I believe that being forty-something affords women of our time a lot of opportunity. In this decade and going forward, we begin to realize that stepping into opportunities is our birthright. We begin to know our personal power, and this changes everything.

When everything comes apart, it is the most wondrous opportunity for you to recreate your life just as you really want it to be!

But sometimes the path to the winner's circle feels like failure. Sometimes life just seems to beat you up. That's it—straight, no chaser—and you probably already know this. The first noble truth of Buddhism is that all life is suffering. Our suffering is usually in proportion to our desire for things, situations, and people to remain the same. As we learn to flow with the inevitable changes that go with life, we will suffer less and find more intrinsic peace and joy. In order to accomplish that, you must achieve a level of mastery you may feel is out of reach. And so here, in this book, I offer tools that will help you achieve that mastery: having clarity, confidence, and courage as you move through life.

Introduction

This book is for any woman in her forties who could use some encouragement and validation that you are enough, and that you can bounce back from anything that temporarily knocked you down, shook your confidence, and left you doubting yourself. As your life coach I will be reminding you that you are enough. You have only to own it and share your authentic brilliance with the rest of us.

I wrote this book as a guide for others along their journeys and also as part of my spiritual practice. I've begun to recognize the insight that comes from self-observation and truth-telling. These activities put us in contact with who we really are, which is the most spiritual way to be. We come to know the divine as it dwells within us when we see ourselves in action. The observer, or higher self, is always present, living this life with us. It *is* us, in a nonphysical, ethereal kind of way, guiding, inspiring, waking us up on time even when the alarm didn't go off, reminding us of that computer password we can't seem to recall, and telling us to call that friend, who just so happened to be thinking of us, too.

I understand life to have greater significance than just what the eye can see. I believe that we are all here as part of something larger, and that our expansion is part and parcel of that larger being. We are never alone on our journeys. We are always accompanied by a divine host of angels, guides, ancestors, or whatever you may call them. That is clear to me because many times in my life I've been certain of some kind of divine intervention. And throughout my forties, I have relied upon my divine connection every day.

Years ago, I named my company Quest For Meaning, not fully realizing that, indeed, the name was my heart's strongest desire— to find meaning. It set me up for my own perfect journey. Likewise, this book is a guidepost so that you can see yourself in your daily activities of living, loving, surviving, thriving, hurting, and wondering through the human experience; bring a spiritual framework to it; and find meaning in your experiences.

That relationship that broke your heart—what was really going on there? That "perfect" job that you lost—what role does this play in your world? The shame of filing bankruptcy—why would you need that experience? The crushing and life-altering pain of losing a loved one—how do you live through and grow from that experience? These questions lead you back into these experiences in a different way. If you can step outside of the experience, you can ask, Who am I and how do these particular experiences actually serve me? If all of these things are just happenstance, then does life have any meaning beyond any particular moment? I believe that life has all the meaning we give it. We start by understanding who we really are: divine beings seeking experience and growth.

Moreover, I look beyond the human ego tricks that try to convince us that we are limited and should be scared. Our lived experiences leave their marks upon our memories, souls, and bodies. However, our spirit says, "*Those* things are temporary; *you* are eternal." I have found much freedom in that insight.

In this radical decade of our forties, women like you and me can begin to put ourselves first and speak our truths.

Radical Lesson #1

Be Open to Growth

In my various roles of speaking, coaching, and teaching, I often advise people on how to successfully navigate the ups and downs of life. The key, I tell them, is to be open to growth. We must remain open to growth because life has so much to teach us. In fact, if we want to enjoy our journeys at all, we should learn to recognize when it is time to grow willingly with ease and grace, because the other option is to be dragged into growth by life's vicissitudes. Growth is a natural progression of life; without it, there is stagnation and death. I believe we are all here to participate in the evolution of things larger than ourselves. Participation means that we are called to be our best selves, to be in the image and likeness of God. To do so, we will stretch ourselves, and it will be uncomfortable sometimes. Spiritual teachers have always told us that growth is unavoidable.

The question is, What will be your teacher? Your ideal attitude is to believe that difficulties can be overcome. Like going to the gym to work out your core, training your spiritual, emotional, and psychological muscles allows you to thrive as you grow. You can become stronger and more fit if you develop a good measure of resilience, self-discipline, and a faith in something larger than yourself.

---

40 Something Nugget of Wisdom

Life offers us many opportunities to step into who we really are.

The decade of our forties is an important station in life because we have a good amount of life experience now, we still have some youthful energy and resilience to face difficulties and recover, and we have at least some degree of maturity to ask ourselves the hard questions about who we have been and who we are on track to becoming. We have the opportunity in our forties to look back over our experiences; honestly come to know our own frailties, insecurities, fears, and dysfunctional coping mechanisms; and decide to do something about them.

Maybe you realize that your career has stalled, and you don't have any passion for it anyway. You're looking at another twenty to twenty-five years of working. Are you going to let the life drain out of you slowly as you put on a fake smile and perform for the public eye? At forty-something, this kind of living is excruciating, but the good news is you still have time to make a major course correction. It's scary as hell to leave what looks like security to venture into the unknown world of following the dream you buried long ago, but what are you going to do—live or die?

I'm here as your example and your coach. I thought losing my "secure job" as a college professor would surely be my undoing, but you know what? It turned out to be a blessing. During my time outside of academia, I grew a whole new set of skills and self-confidence that is unshakable. It's unshakable because it is not based in anything outside of myself. It's based on a strong inner core that now stands and says, "You can do anything." I can tell you this: when shit happens in your life, hold your nose and plant seeds. Your new life can blossom right there in all of that fertilizer.

And in your forties you find out who your real friends are. You will certainly need at least one female friend who has your back, stands by your side, talks you down from the ledge in the middle of the night or middle of a workday, and calls you out when you're hiding, playing small, acting stupid, or not thinking straight. I love how my best friend tells me this, sometimes loudly, sometimes calmly, in casual conversation: "You don't even sound like yourself. You're not thinking straight." I love her! She's also probably the most honest and generous person I know. She models that for me. She has held my hand over multiple breakups and a forty-something life crash, and I have done the same for her when some jackass left her with her wedding dress hanging in the closet. We both bounced back from our disappointments and hurts. You will need your friends. I don't mean those people you just hang out with, chit-chatting over nothing. We are past the point of spending time with pettiness and "frenemies." Get real! Life can be tough, and your real friends will be there to carry you when you can't even walk. You'll do the same for them, and one miraculous day you'll look back on that stuff and laugh.

Rediscovering Yourself

Here's why I would not be twenty-something again. In my view, your twenties are fraught with the high anxiety of trying to discover who you are as an adult human being. You begin to separate from your family identity and norms, and take on burgeoning adult responsibilities, which you often have no idea how to manage. With luck, you have fun in the discovery process. Yes, there can be life trauma—my trauma was my mother dying when I was twenty-one—or you may come from difficult circumstances, but at some point you get your feet under you. You make lots of mistakes, probably indulge in various excesses, and begin to discover yourself, however clumsily. The anxiety comes from the social, cultural, familial, and religious influences and frameworks that shape us all to one degree or another.

At twenty-something you are fresh out of your family's house, brimming with expectations and hope for a great life. The program in your mind may go something like this: "After graduation, I'm going to get a good job, work hard, hang out with my friends, find my husband, and get married by thirty. We'll have a house and two kids by the time I'm thirty-five, and then I'll have a really good position in my company. All will be swell because I'm a nice person, I have a college degree, and everything will work out great!" None of these things may have anything to do with who you are or what you really want, but the thing is, you don't know that yet. You're on autopilot set by your particular combination of influences. Or if you are aware of those influences, you don't have the first clue what to do about them. There just is no substitute for life experience to shows you who you are and teach you what's what. In your twenties you don't have much of that yet.

Because of others' expectations of us and our own self-doubt, we are unaware of our power and have to discover it for ourselves. The twenties are a raucous, challenging time for this discovery. It sets us up for the next stage with slightly less insecurity and more life experience under our belts.

At age thirty, I began a doctoral program. I stepped into this decade full of hope, excitement, and energy. I was happy with my vocational path. I was finally in alignment with myself in that regard, but I was ill-prepared for the emotional upheaval that would come. You see, although my mother had died when I was twenty-one, I had buried that grief without really processing it in a healthy way, and that messiness was starting to come out in my relationships. I mostly liked romantic relationships from afar. I had a thing for unavailable men. I could rotate a few of those at a time and settle on one for a few monogamous years; then it would dissolve, one way or another. This suited me just fine most of the time. The transformation I was in for in this decade would help me balance my emotional self. Dealing with my emotions is probably the thing I hated most.

Other circumstances during my thirties would also provide growth opportunities. I believe that life is always showing us who we are and where we are in our development. Want to know how emotionally mature you are? Watch yourself in relationships. What do you do when you feel scared, rejected, jealous, or neglected? Do you fight fair? Want to know how well-balanced you are? Think about a time when you have suffered a job or income loss. What fears came up, and what did you do about them? And what about those other times when your ego has taken a hit, and you wanted to stay in bed forever or else stab someone to death. Situations like that show you where your growing and healing edges are.

I've come to realize that the reason I have certain experiences is to have a clearer sense of myself. Our interpretations of external events simply reflect where we are within ourselves, in our own consciousness. Getting internet phished to the tune of $6,500 and having my credit free-fall into oblivion were precisely the types of experiences I needed to have. Certain fears could only be confronted and resolved through experience and faith. Faith was a muscle that I needed to strengthen for confidence and resilience so that when I got ready to do something financially outside of my comfort zone, I wouldn't sabotage myself. When it was time for me to step into the next stage of my evolution, I wouldn't cave or play small. Instead, I would step up. Life experience brings perspective along with it. It allows you clarity, breathing space, and even a bit more comfort in discomfort because you know that any moment of unease is only temporary. It too shall pass.

In your thirties you continue to feel quite a bit of anxiety, but by then it is tempered with a little more life experience to offset the constant angst of the twenties. Life is unpredictable, but you learn that every little bump in the road does not have to throw you into dramatic overdrive. Of course, another way to do the thirties, at least the early thirties, is to be in full-on dramatic overdrive from the realization that you don't have the spouse, baby, house, or other things you figured you'd have by now, and you can't clearly see how you are going to become VP of anything by forty. Right around age thirty-three, there can be a mild-to-severe emotional crash as you realize that you are no longer a spring chicken. Maybe you feel pressure to get focused on one thing or another and stay with it. There is still enough cluelessness at this age that you can feel anxious and not quite good enough, but by now you have probably had some successes that keep you hopeful.

You are also beginning to get glimpses of your own identity. This is the greatest gift you can get, although it may come in the form of challenges, problems, heartbreaks, and other upsets. Some things fall apart. They just don't work out. Maybe you married the wrong person, or married for the wrong reasons, and now divorce is looming. Maybe you have dropped out of grad school and feel ridiculous that you're still trying to find yourself. You may realize that you've spent all of your life so far chasing a dream that was not your own. These circumstances will open the pathway to your self-exploration.

By your late thirties, the desire to do meaningful work has been kicked up a notch by the insistent inner voice nudging you toward your authentic self-expression. By the end of the decade, life is not so much about acquiring things as it is about being true to yourself, whoever that may be. You begin to narrow down all those things you were thinking about doing in your twenties to focus on the right things for you to do now. You have a clearer sense of how to focus your creative energy. You've got a blurry image of yourself slowly emerging from the fog. Maybe for the first time in your life, you are paying attention to your inner voice, recognizing its value as your supreme guidance system. You are beginning to trust yourself.

The decade of the forties ushers in a deep dissatisfaction in many women that simply must be addressed. By now you've probably spent the past two decades working like a dog, trying to create your identity through the accumulation of things, degrees, lovers, or devotion to a spouse or children. But wait, something is missing: YOU! What happened to you along the way of living this life? Do you know who you are? This is the moment to embrace vulnerability and radical truth-telling.

Radical Truth-Telling

Radical truth-telling is one of the internal resources of being forty-something. A dangerous, debilitating, heartbreaking kind of lying routinely passes for normal. I'm not saying that most people are chronic liars. I'm talking about when a woman lies to herself.

You're in so much denial that you don't even know you're lying. The dangerous lie is the one you tell yourself so that you can stay in an unhappy relationship or a suffocating job. It's the lie you tell yourself about what you really want out of life. It's the lie you tell other people when they ask how you are and you say, "Fine," but you're really screaming on the inside, choking back tears of fear and frustration, dying a little from a lack of purpose as the years go by. It takes everything you have to hold back the feelings of not being good enough to be promoted, to find a partner, to be the right kind of mother. Many women have been raised and socialized to just keep working hard, doing the right things, smiling, being nice, and looking pretty, so that when we actually try to determine our own truth, we don't know what it is! We've been in the charade of who we are supposed to be too long to know who we really are.

And for women of color, there can be additional burdens related to cultural and societal stereotypes. As a Black woman, I have to think about the layers of my identity and how I am perceived in different environments. For example, professional success for black women requires a constant effort to be assertive without coming across as angry, loud, or undeserving. Finding an authentic self while presenting an "acceptable" self is complicated! The additional work of side-stepping racial and gender stereotypes is a part of daily life for women of color. As a college professor I have to establish authority and credibility in my classroom on the very first day. Some students have never taken a class with a Black woman professor. I set firm standards and expectations on the first day of class and carry it throughout the semester. I establish that we are not friends and that this is work for all of us. By the end of the semester we have mutual respect for each other. There can be a fine line between performance and authenticity, and if we are not careful, we can begin to lose sight of who we really are in light of trying to meet others' expectations.

Well, thankfully in the forties that inauthentic house of cards typically starts to topple. I say "thankfully" because the likely unpleasant fallout of your own personal story is a perfect opportunity for you to uncover yourself and move into your own authenticity. Here's where stuff gets real, because the unimportant stuff falls away—a troubled marriage, a house, a car, superficial friendships, the stuff that usually seems important to who you are. What remains will reflect who you really are.

One way that I know to uncover the real truth, since it is hiding out, is to use the practice of self-observation. Self-observation is a spiritual practice: it takes us into our interior worlds and asks us to peel back the layers between who we really are and who we pretend to be. In moments of self-observation you can catch yourself just as you are about to do that thing you do that sets off the "false" self, the performer. You might tell a little lie, a fib about something, and it seems harmless enough. When you observe yourself in the process, you can interrogate the moment: "Wait, did I just do that? In what ways am I feeling so inadequate that I thought I needed to lie, even slightly?" For example, observe yourself in the moment when you agree to do something that you don't really want to do. Ask yourself, "Why did I just betray myself by overriding my intuition that tells me not to do that? Am I going to feel resentful about this after the fact? Why am I such a people pleaser?" You get the idea.

One of my clients tells a story of being in such a hurry to get to the altar that she ignored the red flags about the man in front of her. It's not that she actually missed them, but in her haste as a forty-seven-year-old woman who was finally getting married, she chose not to look at the number of incidents in which his words and actions didn't line up. She also chose not to honor her intuition that told her that this guy was not the right one for her. This, of course, is not a unique story. Like many women who are unhappily single later in life, the opportunity to finally get married led her to betray herself. From the beginning of the relationship, he had "love bombed" her. He made her the center of his world, flattered her, catered to her every desire, and promised her a future of love, passion, and family. Then he proposed. What woman could resist?

When he began to take longer to return her calls and text messages, she didn't think anything of it. When he began asking her to pay for things, she didn't mind because it was a sign to her that they were sharing responsibilities. When she caught him in a lie of omission about where he had been and with whom, she excused it, not wanting to pressure him about minor things. She thought he was stressed and probably just forgot those details. Eventually, when she discovered his affair with another woman, she was devastated. She had to face the tough questions: How long had he been lying? How long had this younger woman been in the picture? Did he ever really love me, and had he really planned to marry me at all? Was he just playing me and using my money to "love bomb" another woman? How did I miss that he was not who he said he was? Was I desperate? How could this have happened to me?

Her tears flowed; her heart was broken. She questioned every good thing about herself. And then one day, she explained to me later, "All of a sudden, I realized I needed this lesson. I was too needy, and I relied on someone else to make me feel good about myself. I'm so much better off without that guy, but I really wish I had just paid attention to my gut instinct and saved myself all of this heartache. I knew it wasn't right, but I was happy to go along with him anyway. I've learned to trust myself in a whole new way now. I won't be so needy to fall for this again."

Self-observation and self-reflection allow us the moments of clarity we need to call ourselves out for relying on behaviors and belief systems that don't serve us. With regular use, the momentum builds, and it becomes a consistent practice. You learn to always be honest, at least with yourself. Even if you make the same mistakes, you will no longer be able to lie to yourself about your own motivations.

Seeing yourself clearly enables you to value yourself enough to keep from repeating unhealthy patterns. This is a kind of truth-telling that people spend lifetimes trying to avoid. It is much easier to continue in old patterns or blame others than to do the self-reflection necessary to take responsibility for oneself. Many addictions have been formed in efforts to avoid deep emotion or a buried truth. Even when the patterns are painful, they are familiar and have the potential to keep us stuck.

I want you to be brave, seek your inner truth, and have the courage to live it. That's what it means to be open to growth—personally, emotionally, and spiritually.

It's Up to You

If you want to create a life you'll love, know that there is no universal magic formula. You have to make your own way. You have to be open to growth and willing to go through some pain and heartbreak to get to the other side.

Learn to recognize how you handle fear, how you sabotage yourself, and how you hide and deny your truth either out of fear or out of a desire to fit into someone else's vision of who you are. Have a good look, because these are the things that keep you stuck, or just on the verge of breaking through. These things keep you in your shadow life instead of your fulfilled life on your own terms. To transform your life, you'll have to do the work to expand your consciousness and self-awareness. It won't be me or anybody else who does that for you. It will be you, or it won't happen.

Radical Lesson #2

Heal Your Childhood Wounds

The experiences of childhood run deep in us all. Some of us have been wounded through various forms of trauma, but all of us have been shaped by the people who raised us and the circumstances in which we found ourselves. We have all developed behaviors and coping mechanisms as a result of our particular experiences. Life, being the great teacher that it is, continually offers us ample opportunity to recognize ourselves, thus giving us the opportunity to heal, grow, and thrive. However, such opportunities can be easily missed if we remain unconscious of our wounds and how they continue to affect all of our relationships.

People are fond of saying, "Children are resilient; they'll get over it," or "They're too young to remember this." Recent research, however, has found that even in the womb we are negatively affected by highly stressful environments. Severe forms of abuse and neglect in early childhood are notable predictors of conditions such as psychopathic, sociopathic, narcissistic, and borderline personality disorders, to name a few. But what about those of us who were not abused?

---

40 Something Nugget of Wisdom

Often it is necessary to go back and do the cleanup work before you can move forward into healing. Start with your authentic story.

Many of us don't give much thought to how our childhood experiences might still be influencing our lives today. We look to external circumstances to excuse or justify minor antisocial behaviors in others by saying things like, "Wow, that guy has a temper," or "She's so insecure." Or we tell someone, "Lighten up; don't be so serious all the time." We need to be more conscious of how all of us are carrying wounds from childhood. If you can learn to recognize an unhealthy behavior or pattern in your life as having roots in your early years, you can begin to heal.

Lessons from My Childhood

When I did the healing work of clearing out my childhood wounds, I got more clarity about my life and began to live more authentically. My wounds had left me believing I wasn't allowed to speak about my desires or say what I really thought. I needed to heal the little girl who felt shut down from a childhood in which she was told to be quiet and stay out of grown folks' business. I was privy to various family intrigues and gossip, but I was forbidden to speak about them to anybody, ever. I learned early on to be very careful about what I said out loud.

The only place in which I did feel safe to "speak" was in my writing. I was the type of child to read books endlessly and to make up stories and write them in notebooks that my grandmother brought home for me from the store. I used to imagine elaborate stories about princesses and little girls seeking friends and having adventures. What I did not realize is that I was actually writing about my life and my feelings about it. I thought I was just creating characters I could hide behind and tell stories about.

One day I overheard my grandmother talking to someone else about me and my stories; she said, "Poor thing, she doesn't realize that we all know she's writing about herself." I didn't know that my characters were obvious representations of myself. But I realized that it was not safe to express myself. After that, I tried to censor my writing, but I never quite managed to.

I must've filled dozens of those spiral notebooks, and my grandmother kept them all. Over the years, however, they got displaced, and I'm not sure where they ultimately ended up—probably in the trash. Still, it was just like my grandmother to care about what I had to say and keep a record of it for many years. I don't think that my mother ever read my stories. She was busy as a single parent trying to provide for us, and while as an adult I could look back and understand her situation, at the time it was hurtful that she didn't pause long enough to read my writing. I concluded that my voice was just not that important.

By the time I was an adult trying to have relationships, I began to observe the coping mechanisms that I had developed, and how they had become a huge hindrance along my path of self-discovery as I tried to create fulfilling relationships and a professional identity.

Finding my truth has required some excavation from the past, a retracing of my steps back into the world of my childhood to sift and sort the debris from my true self. I returned to my family and the circumstances that helped to shape me. Many times in my life people thought I lived some kind of perfect or charmed life. They see that I grew up in suburban neighborhoods, did well in school, and was a "good girl." Right out of college I had a job in fashion, and then I gave up that career, earned a PhD, and took a teaching position at a good university. I started making pretty good money, writing books, speaking at events, creating my own events, and having my pick of a number of marriage-minded good men along the way (but I was always a runaway bride—more on that later). All so easy and perfect. NOT! Well, those are the bare facts of my life, but no one's life is perfect and without challenge. I stumbled many times over identity and authenticity.

Let's go back to my childhood growing up in nice neighborhoods.

It was the 1970s and 1980s in Cincinnati, Ohio. We lived in the suburbs, moving frequently but always to good neighborhoods where no one worried about crime or drugs. There were good schools and tree-lined streets, and people seemed content. We had a middle-class lifestyle with plenty of material things, but what was not so obvious was that often we had very little cash on hand. On occasion the phone would get cut off for a couple of days.

I remember clearly one day when I was about sixteen years old and sitting in the kitchen of our rented house, on the phone with a boy I had been getting to know. Mind you, I was the shy girl who rarely spoke to any guys, and I had no idea about boyfriends, but I met this one when I was out at the mall with my best friend. He lived in Dayton, which is about forty-five minutes from where I lived in Cincinnati, so we rarely saw each other and only spoke on the phone occasionally.

I was talking to him (about what, I can't imagine) when suddenly the phone went dead. I didn't know what to do at first, but it was a special occasion to get a call from him, so I wanted to do something. I got on my bike and rode to my grandmother's house to use her phone. I didn't think she would be home, but she usually left the side door unlocked. I pedaled up Grandma's driveway, leaned my bike against the front of the house, and tried the side door—and it was open. But wait, I didn't have permission to make a long-distance call from her phone. I would get in so much trouble if I made that call. I risked it. I figured I would only talk for a few minutes, just to say a proper good-bye, and let him know that I had not hung up on him. The fallout from Grandma shouldn't be too bad for only a few minutes. When we spoke, he said he figured out what happened because he had tried to call me back. I was mortified. I quickly got off the phone and rode my bike back home. Somehow no one seemed to notice the small charge on the phone bill, and I was able to get away with it.

I moved through school fairly easily as a shy and studious kid. I kept a few friends, but my mother moved us around frequently, so I didn't really develop many lifelong friendships from childhood. In addition to learning that it was not okay to speak freely, I also determined for myself along the way that it was not safe to get emotionally attached to people. I knew that we would not stay in any one place for more than a few years, so I did not get easily or quickly attached to anyone. I know that this has contributed, to some degree at least, to my runaway bride syndrome in my adult life.

My mother, Catherine Thornton Martin Brown, was a gregarious, spontaneous extrovert who might decide to move across town or across the country on a whim. Our family called her a gypsy. We often took spur-of-the-moment trips since she worked for American Airlines, and in a pre-9/11 America, we could easily get on a plane at a moment's notice. She was five foot ten, the color of caramel, and, well, pretty hot. She was the life of any party, the center of any crowd, and frequently followed by a legion of male suitors wherever we went. She could also swear like a sailor, dance all night, and, yes, still make it to work. I, on the other hand, was a bookworm with few friends (a casualty from the aforementioned frequent moves and new schools), who liked to go to the library to read about the religions of the world, write stories, and hang out with older people. I had an extensive interior life. When Mom had parties or dinner guests, which was often, I was a recluse, just trying to read my book while they danced, played bid whist, or listened to R&B records into the night.

My father, LaDon Martin, who went by Don, was a stone's throw away. He and my mother had been divorced for most of my life, but he stayed close by. He had remarried, and along with my stepmother, Connie, had two daughters, Latrice and Alicea. Our time together was sporadic by today's standards of shared custody and blended families, but I felt a consistency about it over the years. Whereas my maternal Thornton family is rather cool and aloof, the Martins are affectionate, which always startled me when I went for visits. It seemed odd to me that people actually hugged each other that much. My father was definitely an eccentric personality and prone to being controlling, and we had our ups and downs, but we worked it out over the years. I credit his absent but persistent presence in my life to my relationship style with men, just a little, not too much. More on that later.

As a quiet child, I found it pretty easy to be the good girl, happy to please all the adults around me. I didn't get in trouble. I was never boy crazy or "fast." My major crush was Michael Jackson, and that kept my teenaged life quite occupied (after all, this was the 1980s and *Thriller* was the biggest-selling, most popular album ever). I was a late bloomer with no interest in dating any of the boring boys in my high school. My mother had to practically force me to go to my high school prom. Nothing about it interested me, but she said I would always regret it if I didn't go. So, being a good girl, I went. Likewise, I did everything that was expected of me and almost nothing that was not. People pleasing paid off then, and all seemed right with the world.

Then in the winter of 1988, my mother died unexpectedly following a routine hysterectomy. I was a junior in college and in no way prepared to deal with life without her. By this time she had remarried and I had grown close to my stepfather of only a few years, Rene Brown. Her sudden death was a debilitating tragedy to my entire family, and we probably never healed quite right after it. As for me, I was completely without a rudder, a compass, or any other device for direction and meaning. I learned to submerge my feelings even more.

I felt that I was on autopilot, that an alter ego had taken over my being so that I could continue living, and I remember the exact moment that she entered my life. It was the day of the funeral and the burial. Because I was refusing to leave my Uncle June's house to go to the church, my grandmother was sent in to drag me from the stairs where I had perched myself midway down, staring at the dingy beige carpet. I had every intention of going to the funeral when I first started down the stairs from the second floor of the house, but before I reached the bottom of the staircase I had decided I couldn't go through with it. The funerary ritual seemed to me utterly absurd, and I couldn't stand another well-meaning person coming up to me, asking how I was doing. I just wanted to scream out, "How do you think I'm doing? Just leave me alone!"

Somehow my grandmother was able to get me out of the house and into the funeral home's limousine. She kept telling me that I had to go, that I had to face it, and that all these people came because they wanted to pay their respects to my mother and our family. This made no sense to me, but I kept my mouth shut and went along numbly to the church and to the grave site.

At some point we returned to my uncle's house, masses of people in tow. By that time I had come to resent their presence. Considering the number of details that I have unconsciously blocked out, it is surprising to me that I remember distinctly the moment when I finally withdrew into myself. My family members were piling out of the limousine and into my uncle's house. Somehow I ended up being the last one left outside. It was February in Ohio and bitterly cold, and I was consumed with the idea that we had just left my mother to be put in the frigid ground forever. Some type of mental split happened at that moment, as I stood frozen at the bottom of the steps leading up to the porch. My coat was unbuttoned, and I had dropped my gloves on the ground. Just as I bent down to pick them up, my Uncle June appeared at the door.

"What are you doing out there?" he asked.

"Nothing," I replied as I walked up the porch steps and into his house. By then I was already a different person. My identity had shifted. The person who had dropped the gloves on the cement steps was not the same person who picked them up and went into the house. Denial had worn off and was replaced by shock and despondence. I went up to my Uncle June's bedroom, where everyone had left their coats lying across the bed. I climbed into the bed and buried myself under the coats of friends and strangers.

I returned to college after the funeral and god-awful burial because, of course, that's what my mother would tell me to do. I was numb and going through the motions of campus life. My pseudo-schizophrenic mental split outside Uncle June's house had provided me with a functioning personality who would allow me to go forward with some semblance of a life, as long as my emotions were kept properly stuffed away. I just knew that if I allowed them their due course that I would either go completely catatonic or just die outright. Death would have been preferable at the time. Instead, I became emotionally numb, and stayed that way for the next ten years. My alter ego allowed me to live life in a quasi-normal yet emotionally stunted way. My true self had been long buried. I lived, worked, had relationships, started graduate school, and seemed perfectly fine.

Eventually, I began to feel the need to heal. I realized that I was still on autopilot. However, at a certain point emotional inauthenticity became a heavy burden. I had a choice: continue being "fine," or dig into the emotional boxes that I had buried within myself and begin to unpack them. This, of course, would be no easy feat. In my early thirties, I decided to start by going to visit my mother's grave, something I had sworn I would never do. I say that I decided, but the truth is that I felt inwardly compelled to go. I've always felt myself to be guided by my own spiritual support team of angels, higher self, God, or the universe. They nudge me along this life, and when I am following that guidance, they keep me aligned with my purpose and highest good. Of course, there have been times in life when I have not felt connected and have not followed the intuitive guidance that came to me. On this occasion, I listened, and traveled from Oakland, to her grave site in Cincinnati. I shared my plans with my stepfather, Rene, with whom I still remained in close contact. He offered to fly from Dallas and meet me in Cincinnati. We stayed with my family, but it was just the two of us who went to the cemetery.

There, for the first time, I saw her headstone, which read: CATHERINE THORNTON BROWN, 1948–1988. It was that dash followed by her final year that was so surreal to me. She had died only about a week after her fortieth birthday. This was my mother, and her earthly life had ended. We had left her in the ground?! I was a bit unnerved and began thinking all kinds of morbid thoughts. I remembered that she had been buried in a hideous pink dress that she would never have worn. I remembered that one of her friends had told me at the funeral to take her diamond jewelry off of her before they close the coffin. Then I began to wonder, What would she look like now, having been buried all this time? I had no way to even imagine, thankfully. How odd that we keep our dead in boxes in the ground like this. I knew that her essence was not in that box in the ground, and I did not come undone while standing there in the cemetery. I knew that I would be okay. I was beginning to heal by acknowledging my emotions and reclaiming myself—but it was only the beginning.

This is my story of how I came to lose my sense of self and identity. I might even say that the old, reticent version of me died along with my mother, and that since then I have had the task of rebuilding my own authentic identity. As I stand at the end of my forties, I am able to reflect on my path of self-discovery and see how it has unfolded up to this point. Here in these pages I share my experiences, including the things that hindered me but ultimately strengthened me to be empowered, clear, confident, and authentic. I'm standing with you as you do the same.

What is your story? Are there fragments of yourself that you have lost or buried somewhere? Can you identify a time when you made a drastic shift in personality or behavior? Why did you make that change? Are you still performing that role? I invite you to think deeply and, with some courage, go into those places that caused you to take on a different identity. What parts of you got left behind? Maybe it is time for you to reclaim those parts, heal them, embrace them, and allow them to be a part of the real you. Maybe it is up to you to extend love, acceptance, and compassion to yourself so that you can feel empowered and revitalized. It's up to you to go back to your childhood self: go get her, and let her know that it is okay for her to fully express herself now. If no one seemed to listen or care before, you can love and value yourself now.

A Note About Therapy

Sometimes it's best to seek professional advice to help guide you through grief or anything else that is blocking you from living with peace and joy. Some wounds are difficult to heal from without help, and events can affect us differently as individuals. If you experienced abuse, neglect, or other hardships in your childhood that you are having trouble healing from, I encourage you to seek assistance from a counselor or therapist. There's no shame in asking for professional help. Therapy has helped many people to face their past with courage and develop the skills to heal themselves.

Radical Lesson #3

Face Your Fears

The first thing we should remember about FEAR is that it really means False Evidence Appearing Real. Most of our fears come from reflections on the past or projections into the future. In both cases, we are not fully present in the moment, and our minds truly run away with us. Healthy fear keeps us safe from danger or injury; it is an instinctual survival mechanism and a reaction to actual external stimuli. But most of us are afraid of imagined scenarios or past events that are no longer relevant. As you look at your life now, in this moment, think of what usually keeps you up at night or causes you unease just by thinking about it. Is this a present moment thing, or is it a projection of dread into the future? What if you could put fear in its place, recognizing that it is not real and that it has no place in the life you are trying to create for yourself? What could you achieve if fear no longer stopped you in your tracks?

From Unemployed to Self-Employed

Many people who know me well say that they can see how my mother shaped who I am. They see that side of me that is self-reliant,

---

40 Something Nugget of Wisdom

Fear will never go away, especially when you are growing and changing, but you can be the one in charge. You hold the key.

---

independent, and always keeps it together. Well, yes and no. Yes, because when there is no alternative, I can either sink or swim; I'm a bit of a workaholic. And yes, I can see how this leads to success in some areas of life because this shows up as drive, determination, and purpose. And yes, those are my mother's words right there, even now. But also no, because sometimes I don't have it together. Hard things happen to me, too, and leave me feeling flattened. What I have learned in this most radical decade is that I am creating my life, and I get to create it the way I want to live it. When things seem really hard, I have a huge opportunity for self-analysis, observation, and new decision-making. If I'm not enjoying my life, I tell myself, "Well then, what's it gonna be? Make a new choice, get ready to look fear and doubt in the eye, and get on with it."

For example, writing this book has been a supreme challenge because I recognized that my mission was to write my life, and I was not prepared to do that. I was feeling a mess and definitely not like a successful woman. I had gone through a couple of years where my life seemed completely upside down in unexpected and uncomfortable ways. I had gone from the success of achieving my doctorate degree and becoming a professor of religion at a liberal arts university in Los Angeles to being unemployed when that position was cut and floundering in my own angst. I could not understand how my life had come crashing down into a ditch. I could not understand what the universe was trying to show me or tell me. I had great resistance to doing anything other than being an academic. My whole identity was wrapped up in being Dr. Martin. I would later realize that this had only been my shadow identity working in my shadow career: in other words, I had been hiding out in academia, where it was safe.

The alternative would have been for me to live a life as a writer, which had always seemed too unstable and financially precarious. I always had it in the back of my mind that I would one day be able to pursue writing as my real passion, but in reality, the security of a "good job" won out, and I kept my other interests simmering on the back burner. The funny thing is that I had created another, rather public identity for myself over the years as a life coach and spiritual teacher known as Dr. Darnise. (The universe is so funny.) I was only comfortable when I was able to be both on my own terms. When the academic door closed, I was in shock. How could this happen? I had all my credentials—I had strong teaching evaluations, publications, the support of my colleagues—and yet it all fell away like smoke and mirrors. I had done everything right. I was at a loss. I was confused and angry. And then I began to remember something.

In the past I had spoken of my life's mission as being much larger than a college classroom. For years I had understood my mission to be bigger and broader, like that of a Wayne Dyer or an Iyanla Vanzant. I felt that I had a calling. I had a lofty vision for myself as a writer and spiritual teacher who would make a large impact on the world, but when it came time for me to actually step into that role, I was confused and terrified. Part of the reason for my confusion and fear was that I could not see from that low point how or where to go exactly. It seemed to me that if life had presented me with a clear path detailing how to get from where I was to my lofty goals, I would've been much happier and certain. Of course, the universe does not work this way. It really does not care about our comfort. In fact, the lessons that the universe provides for us leave us anywhere but comfortable.

For me, this time of vocational uncertainty and confusion felt unfair and torturous. It also put me in direct contact with all of my what ifs and insecurities, and I did not care to engage with any of them at all. All of my hang-ups around keeping the perfect facade and being that woman who always has everything together came flaring up at me like a fiery dragon. I imagined that people would see me as a colossal failure. During the first year of my post-academic career I swear I could feel the heat of the dragon's breath on the back of my neck. It nearly did me in. The positive lesson only began to show its face around the two-year mark. It became clearer to me that, indeed, my platform as a life coach and spiritual leader was my true vocation. I began to recognize myself as not unemployed but self-employed. The new vocation would require me to become visible in the world. It would require that I allow my vulnerabilities to show. I had previously attempted to reach people with my intellect, but I began to realize that, in order to help people, I needed to be seen as relatable.

Getting Unstuck

Our unprocessed feelings can keep us stuck in surprising ways. Sometimes those feelings are a result of a relationship that left us feeling inadequate and hurting. Oftentimes, we get stuck because we are afraid. We are afraid to do something that might end up causing the same pain we have experienced before, so we simply shut down and carry on with life in the safe lane. Anytime someone is working with me and saying that they are stuck, I immediately know that they have some kind of unprocessed fear. As counterintuitive as it may seem, people often choose to stay in confusion rather than make a decision and take an action that might turn out to be in the wrong direction.

When going through difficult life events, what we usually miss is how perfectly precise those situations are for us. If you have a fear of never having enough money, you will make unhealthy financial and professional choices. If you have a fear of rejection or abandonment, you will attract partners who will reject and abandon you. Instead of railing against the unfairness of it all, sit with yourself, gather your wits, put on your big girl panties, and ask yourself, What do these experiences reveal about me? Don't worry: we all have something that sends us over the edge or causes us to retreat and lick our wounds. You have enough wherewithal and life experience to face your fears. You can learn to tell if you are manufacturing a fear in your own mind or if there is clear and present danger that needs your attention. You have discernment, and that's really the point.

Think about what scares the bejeezus out of you. I've learned to recognize my underlying fear as the Scarcity Monster. He's been with me for many years, and probably stems back to watching my mother worry about how to pay one bill or another. Scarcity is that feeling that you are running out of something and that it will not be replaced. It can create anxiety, panic, and desperation as you watch your checkbook balance fall too low or experience the end of a relationship—just two examples of what can cause scarcity fear.

A scarcity mindset will take you into places of fear around not having enough, but more importantly it can make you feel like *you* are not enough. And it is a dream killer, because when the fear of scarcity takes up real estate in your mind, you will shrink back from the big vision, from risk, from stepping onto the larger platform. It will make you stop dead in your tracks because you just can't see how there will be enough of this or that. You can't see that you have everything you need to take the big step romantically or financially. It will steal your joy and your peace of mind.

My Scarcity Monster is an enormous, hideous, fire-breathing dragon who likes to singe the hair on the back of my neck every so often. When I let him get the best of me, I hoard every penny I get, refusing to invest in my business or anything beyond paying the rent. He will cause me to think that I will die as a beggar in the street unless I do the practical, realistic thing like get a "real" job like other people do. When I think of expanding my business, buying new video equipment, joining a professional organization, or buying a new dress for my fancy Hollywood life, Scarcity Monster jumps up and tries to burn my eyebrows off! I once bought two dresses for the NAACP Image Awards. Those dresses probably cost about $700 or so—a lot of money for me at the time. I would have liked to have died handing over my credit card. But hey, I was going to be on the red carpet, as I do sometimes, and I needed to invest in myself. In handing over that card, I talked down the monster who threatened me every minute with images of being in the poorhouse. I decided that if that's what happens, I'll be the one wearing those two fabulous dresses for the rest of my life.

If you're thinking, "But I don't think I could do it. My situation is different, and I'm terrified that something bad or humiliating will actually happen!," I understand. My advice to you is this: pull out your credit card! By that I mean, take the step: do one thing that puts you more in alignment with where you want to go. Your situation may not literally require a credit card, but do the next thing that seems too scary. Even a small step in the right direction will begin to diminish the fear and make it manageable as you keep moving.

If your goal has been simmering on the back burner for years, then you know that it is real and true for you. Be willing to take chances and move through challenges. As long as you can eat and keep a roof over your head, invest in yourself!

Sandy's Story

Let's meet Sandy. She is in her early fifties and has a professional career, but she has a dream to open her own wellness business. She has many certifications and lots of knowledge but only provides massage and facial services to friends and friends of friends. Sandy keeps everything low key, unofficial. However, she comes to work with me because she feels very frustrated that she does not seem to be able to turn her hobby into a real business. Every time she seems to make some headway and gain some momentum, something in life pops up requiring her time, energy, and money. Her business withers, and she has to start all over again. She is tired of this pattern but doesn't know what to do about it.

Here's an excerpt from one of our coaching sessions:

Me: Sandy, what feelings come up for you when someone asks to book a massage with you?

Sandy: I feel happy at first. Then I worry and think that I shouldn't have accepted it. I feel like I will only disappoint them.

Me: Why do you worry that you will disappoint them?

Sandy: Because they are going to realize that I'm not that good, not as good as others. That's why I charge so low too. At least they won't feel like they wasted much money.

Me: But you've told me that people want to continue seeing you, and they ask when you're going to do it full-time, so that must mean something, right?

Sandy: Yes, but I get scared, like something in my throat is tight and swollen. I start telling people that I'm unavailable so they'll stop asking me.

Me: Then how do you feel, once people stop asking you?

Sandy: Initially, I feel relieved. Then I feel mad at myself for stopping again. I get caught in my cycle.

Me: What if you just kept going, despite your fear, and kept accepting appointments? What if you just need to work through nerves? Could you think about it that way?

Sandy: No, because I know that it's not nerves. It's me. I feel like something is welling up inside of me, trying to come out. I guess I'm holding it in, and that's why my throat feels like I have a ball stuck in it. I can't bring myself to let it out even though it gets literally hard to breathe.

Me: So this feeling comes up inside of you when your business starts picking up?

Sandy: Yes, and then I shut it down, and I feel some kind of relief, which only turns into frustration. But I can deal with that better, I guess.

ME: Are you willing to find out what that something is that keeps trying to well up and come out? You can see that it is blocking your business momentum, right?

SANDY: I'm getting scared just thinking about it. But that's why I'm working with you, to get past these blocks. I would never have thought that opening my business would bring up my emotional stuff. That's kind of a trip!

ME: Yep, the universe is a trip. It's very precise in knowing just how to help us move forward. That fear and tightness in your throat is a gift to you. It has brought your attention to wounds you've been carrying. See how that works? What is the truth that you need to know about yourself here?

SANDY: I have to realize my sense of inadequacy. Of course I could trace that to my childhood, but I can see that regardless of where it comes from, I have to make the change in the present. I often felt like I didn't belong anywhere as I was growing up, so I felt like something was wrong with me. When I did make friends, I was afraid they would find out that I wasn't really like them or something. . . . I'm not even sure what I feared. Anyway, I see I'm still living like that, and it's keeping me stuck.

After a few sessions with Sandy, it was clear to me that she couldn't move forward with her dream because of her fears. She was afraid of being visible and thus open to possible criticism and rejection. Although she was a healer, she still had healing to do within herself. She knew that undertaking such healing would require significant therapeutic self-work. She didn't want to deal with the emotional baggage that she had been keeping a lid on for over twenty years. Because she'd been actively avoiding her own processing and healing, she had unconscious resistance to fully walking with others through their healing. On the surface she very much wanted a flourishing wellness business, but she was unaware of how she had been hiding from her own pain. That hiding behavior caused her to unknowingly sabotage her attempts to start her business. On a certain level, she knew that walking others through their own healing would make it impossible to avoid her own healing process. The latent pain of reopening wounds controlled her ability to make progress in her business.

She did not see this at first. It was hard for her to see the connection between feeling like an outsider, shame around decisions she had made to be accepted and loved, deep feelings of unworthiness, and how those things blocked her from being able to believe in herself enough to get paid to give massages and facials. Her symptoms were pretty clear and easy for me to read, but since she was hiding from her truth, she couldn't see the connection. The scared part of her did not want to see it, but the larger part of her, the one with a vision who came into this life to shine, would not let her rest. Eventually the cycle of starting and stopping her business became too frustrating to deal with yet again.

I coached Sandy for many sessions. She also did energy work with a Reiki practitioner. Her outcome was that she forgave herself for what she considered shameful behavior of an insecure girl, and she started to rebuild her self-worth. I challenged her all along to accept as many requests as she could for her services as a barometer to see where she was with herself. Since she was also doing her own self work, I believed that she could push through her discomfort and resistance. Now that she knew what that anxiety was connected to, she could build her confidence by talking herself through it and developing her business at the same time.

The lesson: don't allow yourself to stop at challenging circumstances. See obstacles as manifestations of your own fear and procrastination. Gee, it's awfully convenient that a dental bill came up, and now you have to spend $500 that you were going to use to invest in your website. Don't let yourself off the hook; how else can you still make it happen? Dig into why you are having this manifestation. It really didn't "just happen." Is it serving you or hindering you? Be diligent and tell yourself the truth about it until you get to pay dirt. You'll know when you get there because it will really ring true, and there may even be tears as you recognize the depth and breadth of the stuff you have been holding on to, as well as the scope of influence it has had over multiple aspects of your life.

Fear and Relationships

Fear can play a big role in how we behave in intimate relationships. The relationship in my adult life that ended up being extremely meaningful and pivotal was with Bill, who challenged me beyond belief. I met him in December 2010 at the birthday party of a local Los Angeles politician. Bill stands out in any room because he is six foot four; he is also a well-known actor and director. We started talking, and despite our twenty-four-year age gap, I was smitten, and we began an immediate courtship, which turned into a dramatic relationship.

Bill has had a lot of success in his career, and he has rightfully reached the stage of icon. That meant that our relationship would necessarily revolve around the machinations of his profession. What I didn't realize at first was how much my personal interests and goals would have to take a backseat to his. Nor did I realize how much emotional growth I would experience and interior clarity I would gain.

Being in authentic relationship with Bill meant that I had to stretch into the most uncomfortable and downright painful places of my emotional being. This is what is called for in *real* relationships, not casual ones. After years of dating multiple men casually, or just never investing myself fully, I stated my intention to the universe that I wanted to walk in mastery and that I wanted a *real* relationship, and then all hell broke loose in my life. That may seem to be a strong and even negative way to describe a romantic relationship, but the truth is, I realized I was going to have to step into all of those emotional places that I had actively avoided all of my life. I was now on the hook, so to speak, to engage my fears around vulnerability, security, and abandonment. I fought and resisted the man in front of me—not because he consciously challenged me, but because those fears were underneath the topics we fought about, at least on my end.

I was in a situation in which my identity was shifting in just about every aspect of my being. I had just lost my job, and I had not found a new one. I was scared and felt insecure about my finances and lifestyle. I had asked the universe for mastery, and I was getting my master class in every aspect of my life all at once! I felt that the rug had been pulled from under my feet, upsetting my entire life, and here was this relationship that demanded that I do the very things I hated the most: be vulnerable, don't resist, let someone else help, let my guard down. Well, initially I was having none of it. And by initially, I mean for at least a year! The relationship was difficult, and Bill had his own issues, so we had breakdowns, breakups, and arguments. But when I had a moment to put things into the larger spiritual perspective, I realized what was going on. I was having the perfect opportunity to learn to face down my fears. I had to overcome them by facing them head-on. All of my stuff came up, security and ego being the primary ones, and they were doozies for me! The things that I had used to create an identity and an image were gone. Now what would I do?

Late one Christmas Eve, Bill and I had an argument that lasted into the wee hours of Christmas Day. I can't even remember what it was about. I'm sure it was something rather insignificant that got blown out of proportion and beyond reason, as usual. I didn't sleep at all. I was furious. I was hurt, and I was at the end of my rope with trying to get this man to really see and hear me. All I wanted to do was leave his house, go home, get in my bed, and cry my eyes out over the failure that my life had become. But I had promised not to run out on him again in the heat of an argument. I had made a commitment to stay and try to work things out, and it was Christmas Day, for God's sake. I couldn't make a scene on Christmas.

In the morning, I had a long, hard conversation with my spiritual advisor, Rev. Q, by phone. Thank God he made himself available on Christmas; otherwise I don't know what I would have done. He told me straight away, "Look, nobody has a gun to your head forcing you to stay. If you really need to go, GO! Forget what anybody else thinks." I said I knew deep down that leaving would mean avoiding a truth I needed, and so I would stay and try to sort myself out. He then helped me see the bigger picture, asking me, "Are you in mastery right now, or are you allowing a circumstance to lay you out? You have got to master this, and you can do it. The path is not easy, but you *can* do it."

The conversation went on for some time, with me sequestered in the bedroom, avoiding the morning activities. I hadn't even called my own family to wish them a merry Christmas. Eventually, Bill came back into the room and got in on the conversation as it turned to relationship issues. I felt he had softened a bit, and after the call I could at least put one foot in front of the other. The day unfolded with his family and friends, food and gifts, but the truth in my gut told me that we were on borrowed time.

By the next day, back in my own apartment, I was still emotional and feeling scared, but I was not lying on the floor wanting to hide from my life. Then my best friend called me. By the time she talked some sense into me, reminding me of who I really was, I felt I was finally seeing the light at the end of a dark, scary, lonely tunnel. It was a glimmer, but it was enough. I had a major shift. I could see the divine plan operating in my circumstance. I was not doomed. I was not a failure. I had people around me who were helping me. All I needed to do was let them in. A burden had been lifted. What had made the difference? Recognizing what my core fears really were, facing them, realizing that they were not as bad as I had thought, and allowing my faith to grow where that fear had been. I spent days and nights in prayer, and I felt supported.

I wish I could say this was an easy process, or that it will be easy for you, but I can't. What I know for sure is that we all have core fears that show up in our lives. They make up the biggest, most hideous fire-breathing dragons you can imagine scaring the bejeezus out of you. The process of recognizing fear is very precise, made to order, just for you. In order to grow, you must face your fear. Now you can choose not to face it, but therein lies the rub. There will be no growth, no forward progression for your life. You will be stuck and wondering why you cannot get ahead, why you cannot finish the things you start. It will seem unfair. You will feel like a victim, like a failure, or like life is just hard and doing you wrong. Your circumstances will be difficult and unfulfilling. You will begin to resent others and begrudge them their happiness and successes, because you want some for yourself but seem unable to get any.

And do you know what is keeping you there? *Your fear!* It will stop you every time you try to take that big step or do that risky thing that doesn't make sense to anyone but you. You will be afraid of what others will think. You will be afraid of failing and looking foolish for deciding to quit your job or walk away from a relationship. Honestly, most people will stop here. They will give up on themselves because it is too scary to step away from the devil they know. Change can be terrifying, and falling back into an old default mode is easier than creating new habits. But the truth is having something different requires doing something different. It is really that simple.

I look at my life, and specifically that Christmas Day transformation, and I see my shift. It was the day my ego was crucified and a more authentic me was resurrected. I see that I finally had to let go of my own resistance and just allow myself to be vulnerable. There really was no other option at that point. I had done everything I knew how to do, and nothing was working. It would have been easier if I had just gotten that wisdom nugget earlier in my process. I might not have spent so much energy kicking and screaming and feeling like I was being dragged by my hair by the big, scary dragon into no-man's-land to be painfully killed and devoured. Instead of just surrendering, I had to have a knock-down, drag-out fight with myself.

This resistance is the ego acting out, and it is vicious. Its job is to protect us from annihilation. It is not all bad. It is helpful for avoiding hot stoves and slippery cliffs and rattlesnakes. It drives us to find food and shelter. The real problem with the ego is that it thinks it is in charge, and it is afraid of its own annihilation, which is really just our awakening out of fear. As we awaken to a higher consciousness, we see the ego for what it is. We can keep it in perspective and understand its shenanigans and tantrums. They are the stuff of illusion.

The great lie of existence is that we are alone in the cosmos and must fight to the death for our sustenance and very being. This is not true, but the ego thrives on our belief that it is. Consequently, the moment you stretch to do something unknown, risky, or different, like ending a relationship that isn't working, the ego perceives this as a threat to existence and thus acts up. Enter your very own personalized dragon! If you have the higher consciousness to understand what is happening, you do not panic. You understand and trust the process. The light can illuminate the darkness.

Insights from Iyanla

When you are in pain, afraid, or panicking, you make bad decisions. You forget your own power, and you begin to lean too heavily on what others have to say about you and your life. Assess your situation. Is it truly bad, or are you just telling yourself that it is or will be bad? The facts may be beyond your control, but the conclusions are yours to draw and own. If you are afraid that you will lose your job or your car will be repossessed or you will lose your house, it may be true that those things could happen. But if you add on to this collection of realistic possibilities that you are a failure and no one loves you or ever will, you've now created a conclusion to those events that are not, in fact, true.

Falling on hard times or losing something that was valued or loved is difficult, and it may hurt your feelings, but you don't have to beat yourself up with generalized assaults to your soul. Be gentle with yourself, especially when you are already scared to death. This is the time to use your best spiritual tools, resources, and best friends to help you keep your head above water and thinking clearly.

If you cannot muster any of these things, and let's face it, sometimes you just cannot, then do nothing. Get still and quiet with yourself and ask for divine help. Pray for assistance, and then wait for signs to come to you in the form of songs on the radio, something on TV, a conversation with a coworker, or an encounter with a stranger. The universe will respond, but you must be able and willing to hear your message. The message will be your salvation through that crisis. Listen and do nothing else until you get a nudge to make a move. Then follow the guidance you get.

In the midst of fear and panic, I learned that the greatest strength can come from a willingness to be vulnerable. Iyanla Vanzant's book *Peace from Broken Pieces* gave me that insight. It is an amazingly honest story of her life and her shortcomings, but mostly her longing for love given her extremely abusive and neglectful childhood. While my circumstances have not been so severe, I can relate to feeling abandoned, neglected, unwanted, and uncared for. My response has been to protect myself from getting too attached to people by keeping a pretty good wall up.

I don't love 100 percent of myself, and I probably don't even expect others to love me completely. At some point along the way I decided to protect myself against potential abandonment. People you love will die. I have lost so many people I care about that I can hardly bear it, and each time my determination to protect myself became even stronger. When I was with Bill, I pulled back because of the increased likelihood that I would have to face his death. (Even now it's hard to even write that!) Over the years he felt a sense of distance or limitation from me. And I from him, because relationships are always a reflection. Unfortunately, he interpreted my distance to be a lack of love and caring, but in fact it was my defense mechanism. Whereas some people deal with their fear of abandonment by latching onto others, I erect an invisible wall. If I don't get too close, I don't get too hurt. Perfect arrangement, right?

Beyond reading Iyanla's book, I also got to know her personally and benefitted from her insights. She's identified certain behaviors and patterns in my life, giving me a lens by which to see and better understand myself. On more than one occasion she personally called me out for "playing small," but at the time I couldn't even understand what she meant. I was in so much denial and uncertainty that even when called on the carpet, I was clueless. I desperately needed that light to shine into the crevices and hiding places of my life. These particular behaviors and beliefs were natural to me because I had been living with them since childhood. They had become my way of life, and now they needed to be dismantled if I was going to live into my truth and fullness.

Here are some lessons for forty-something growth that I learned from her:

(1) Pretending everything is okay when it is not is like a poison. If ever you are stifling your truth, it will manifest in other ways, like physical illness; relationships that don't work out; general, "free-floating" anxiety; and the like.

(2) Being unwilling to name something for what it is can keep you stuck. If you are in an abusive situation but look for other ways to describe it, then this lesson is about you. I was unwilling to acknowledge that I let other people's agendas alter my own. I lost myself for a while because of it. When something is harmful or even toxic, name it!

(3) Similarly, not being authentically yourself will keep you from growing. Finding myself again became priority number one so that I did not fall into other people's ideas about who I am. Because of lack of clarity on my part, I substituted other people's thoughts and plans for me in place of my own.

I know that it's challenging to face your fears. But you know what else? Moving through these fierce shadows is necessary. It is the price you will pay along the way to your wholeness, wellness, and successes. The Scarcity Monster still tries to come for me, but he doesn't live with me anymore. He acts up, and I put him out. Remember that fear only appears real. You give it life and energy by allowing it to shut down your momentum and dreams. There comes a time, and forty-something is a great time, when you have to make a decision and take an action in the direction you want to go. Even when things seem to go terribly wrong, there is an aftermath—let's call it an afterglow. You will have strengthened your resiliency muscles, and fear will be that much weaker. Courage does not mean waiting until fear subsides; it means doing the thing anyway. Onward!

Radical Lesson #4

Identify Your Values and Priorities

I have been known to do a little matchmaking. I don't do it often, but on occasion it occurs to me that I know two people who might get on well together. The way I come to this conclusion is by looking at shared core values and priorities. When I know that the individuals are similar types of people, then I know that I am onto something. For example, in one case the individuals were both educators, writers, social justice advocates, artists, and smart people who were each interested in finding a partner for marriage and having children. They were a good match at the time based on their core values and priorities.

Do you know your own values and priorities? Begin with the questions, Who am I and what do I want most in my life right now? If I tell the truth about myself, what might need to change in my life? This is no small matter and no quick exercise for most of us, because we are not used to looking at ourselves this way. We always seek to put our best face forward, and thus we may even forget our

---

40 Something Nugget of Wisdom

If you can name your core values and try to live by them, your life will be in alignment. If you let others' values guide you, you will be out of alignment.

---

real likes, wants, and needs. Once it becomes clear, for example, that you value family life above any other lifestyle focus, that clarity can help you sort out incompatible friends and lovers who value a more work-driven lifestyle. If you know that you need alone time as part of your own self-care routine, then you will not overextend yourself by saying yes to others when you really need to say no, even if it is just to stay home and watch the Home Shopping Network. At this point in our lives we have likely had experiences where we did not hold fast to our own values, if we even knew them, and we have suffered the consequences. We have poured ourselves out chasing something or someone, only to end up resentful and angry at them, and angry with ourselves, because we knew better deep down. Now that you have that wisdom, you can move through the world rooted more firmly in your own core values, and be more willing to release things that don't serve your highest good.

Usually, pain, suffering, or some kind of unwanted circumstances push us to come to a crossroads and make new choices. This is a manifestation of the gap between living according to one's values and priorities and living according to some other plan. This dissonance is all too common and will lead to frustration and pain. In my case the pain was in feeling I had not quite lived up to my potential. So I would work really hard and try to be available to others, even when I didn't want to. I created these scenarios in which I ended up abandoning my own priorities, doing things I didn't want to do because I worried about what people thought of me. I don't want to disappoint them or cause them to not like me or to see me as a difficult person who was not a team player. I was living as a people pleaser, and I couldn't even identify my own values.

Only at forty-something did I come to any consciousness about this problem. I could see it in others quite well, but not in myself. I finally started to reevaluate my life priorities because it had become too painful to continue living that way. I had lost track of myself and any sense of guidance for how to get where I actually wanted to go. So now, I came to a full stop and asked, Who am I and what do I want?

Saying Yes Instead of No

I answered this question with a trip to Tanzania. While I was working at the university, a colleague offered me a free trip to Tanzania to volunteer at a village school and go on a safari. For me the trip was painful in many ways and a revelatory growth experience. Finding myself in the midst of discomfort and angst, I had to ask myself how I even came to be there. Why had I come to Tanzania under circumstances that put me in a position to do nothing but what I didn't want to do? Contrary to the others I traveled with, I did not have any lofty goals about volunteering and making a difference in Africa. I did not desire to challenge myself in that way. I had to admit that the only reason I'd agreed to come was because a colleague asked me to, and I felt I would disappoint her if I said no. I was trying to do what I thought I should want to do, but secretly I did not want to go. I worried that my colleague would think less of me if I did not take this golden opportunity. Rationally, I know that she was not likely to think any less of me, but in my mind I believed it was possible.

But who says no to a free trip to Africa? How could I not be grateful for the opportunity and excited to have that experience? Well, the truth is that I did not want that experience, at least not in the way it came, accompanying a group of college students with whom I would live in a hostel and work in a small village school. Anyone who knows me well can tell you that none of that sounds like anything I would ordinarily choose to do. I enjoy going on vacations with upscale accommodations and don't find it appealing to go on a safari that includes sleeping in a tent on the ground surrounded by roaming, large, wild animals. Nope, that is decidedly not who I am in this lifetime. The truth is that I should have said thanks for the invitation, but no thanks, it's not for me. What came out of my mouth was "Sure, I can do that."

I know now that I had slipped into people-pleasing mode; I wanted to be perceived as a team player at the university where I taught. I really respected the person asking me, and I felt obligated to say yes. She didn't pressure me in any way, but I gave in to my sense of needing to prove myself. Of course I had some good experiences while in Tanzania, and I met some amazing people who taught me all kinds of lessons about resiliency and unconditional love in the toughest of circumstances. But most of all, I learned about myself. That's the real gem that I take away from that thirty-day trial by fire. Little did I know that it was just one of my life experiences that would show me myself. That trip was the doorway into a three-year period of trial-by-fire truth-telling and coming to know, value, and trust myself.

I realized that there were many occasions when I had ended up spending my time and money doing things that other people thought would be good for me to do. They weren't asking maliciously but sometimes selfishly for their own benefit or advantage. I say that knowing that we all act for our own benefit. But in these cases, again, I substituted other people's judgment for my own. I believed that they knew better because they seemed further along the pathway to success than I was or had more money than I did, so I was inclined to follow their lead, always hoping that it would lead to my own success. I thought there was a magic pill that would transform my life into something big and grand. The trouble with that kind of thinking is that I followed external things and other people, forsaking myself.

I've spent thousands of dollars and years of my life looking outside of myself for the answers to what I really want: peace, love, joy, wealth. Yes, I have managed to get it down to these four words. The path I have now decided to take is surrendering to the next stage of my evolution, getting off the wheel of other people's expectations, and eagerly expecting the next shift in my life to be both life-altering and good.

You see, I've learned something since the last time I went through this kind of shift, nearly twenty years ago. I've learned that it is better to go with it, that I shouldn't resist it out of fear and trepidation. The change is already here; resistance is futile. One can go either kicking and screaming, or in peace and faith knowing that all is well. This time I will go in peace and faith right from the start.

Lessons from Mom

I've gotten good at persisting despite the challenges, getting refocused as necessary, and carrying on. My mother's influence has been the most critical component in my journey. She was a no-nonsense kind of parent who did not accept anything less than my best. She set the bar high and demanded that I reach it, no matter how young I was. When I would complain and say that something was "too hard," she would say, "I didn't ask you if it was hard. Do it anyway!" She was not a touchy-feely, nurturing kind of mother. She was not big on the hugs, kisses, "I love yous," pats on the back, or appearances to cheer me on. She would go over my report card with a fine-tooth comb and point out my dismal math performance, no matter how well I did in English, history, and Spanish.

She did see my talent for writing early on and encouraged it. When I was looking at colleges and trying to pick a major, she told me that I should be a lawyer or a teacher. She was right, but of course I did not listen then, and went off to study fashion in preparation for my fabulous career as a fashion executive. But later I returned to subjects I loved—writing, history, religion—and I became a university professor.

One of the most important lessons I learned from my mother came through losing her. Just before the surgery that ultimately ended her life, she began to talk about wanting to do something different with her life. She no longer wanted to be an airline employee. Her heart longed to do something else. She did not know what exactly, but she was ready to lean in a new direction. I knew that she felt stunted by her job. Even though she had taken different types of jobs at American Airlines—phone reservationist, airport agent, even roles in different cities—ultimately none of them allowed her to feel fulfilled. I knew that she felt locked into her job because of the security, ability to provide for me, and the travel perks, but I also saw her call in sick some days saying, "I just can't do it today."

I saw her come home from work many days with the same ritual: walk straight to the bathroom, disrobe down to her panties, and walk nearly naked through our house to her bedroom. Her uniform would be left in a heap on the floor: navy blue work pumps; navy blue pantyhose; navy blue skirt and blazer; white shirt with American Airlines emblem; red, white and blue scarf; and her bra; all deliberately discarded. Then she would say to me, "Bring my uniform in here." In a huff because she didn't just carry her own clothes with her, I would gather up all of her clothes, which still carried the scent of her perfume, and take them to her room. Her fragrance always lingered in the air long after she left a room.

What I initially internalized from watching my mother struggle and work at an energy-sucking job was that life is hard, having a child is hard, and that means you will have to sacrifice your soul. In creating that story, I determined that I was a burden to her and needed to make sure I did everything right so that she would be happier. Somewhere along the line I decided that I wouldn't be having any children. I knew that my grandmother had worked hard to raise her seven kids, and I saw my mother doing unfulfilling work and yearning for another way of life.

What I also learned from observing my mother is the importance of making space and time for that which sustains you and makes you happy. She hadn't quite figured out how she could be true to herself and earn a living, but the calling was welling up inside of her. I was off in my sophomore year at Kent State, and she was in her second marriage. She finally had enough breathing room to think of her own next episode. Unfortunately, she ran out of time at forty years and one week of age. She was at the precipice of her most radical decade, in which, I am sure, she was set to do some amazing stuff. Reflecting on her life and her entry into her forties, I know that she was onto something for herself. When I entered my forties, I wanted to make sure I took advantage of the opportunities she never got to have.

Working to Live, Not Living to Work

Now that you are spending some time on your identity, let's think about your vocation—not just the work you do for money, but the work that aligns with who you truly are. Have you had a job that you truly hated? I certainly have, and it was miserable. The good thing is that the misery is your sign to make a move. Spirit does not call you to remain in misery; it nudges you to make a new choice and take a new action, scary and uncertain as that may be.

Aside from love and relationships, a lot of my clients come to me because they are at a crossroads in life about vocation and purpose. They wonder aloud, "Is this all there is to my life?" Then I begin a process of helping them rediscover their deepest truths, reclaim their innate talents and skills, and reconnect to their most intimate dreams. Happiness is being able to make a joyful living doing what you love.

In my case, three years after I lost my teaching position, the university called me back to work there again. It seems that once I made peace with myself about my multiple professional identities, my vocation and purpose, and my self-value, opportunities began to open up for me again. I had learned to be resourceful during my time away from teaching. I had taken that job loss very hard, because I had over-invested myself in a place that really had not invested in me, much to my surprise and dismay. At the time it all fell apart, I felt that the institution and people I had known for years failed me, and I was hurt and angry about it for a long time. I eventually realized, however, that I'd needed to have my status quo disturbed. I was, in fact, getting too comfortable with the academic life, and losing my focus on my true purpose. In addition, and perhaps more importantly, I found out there were a good many skills I had yet to develop that I would need in my life as an entrepreneur and that would not be gained in a college classroom.

I had always thought of myself as an independent woman, fully capable of taking care of myself all of my adult life. But it really was not until I had a come-to-Jesus, bottom-falling-out type of experience that I really knew myself as independent. One thing I learned is that being independent does not mean that you never need help. I learned how to ask for help and how to receive it when it is offered without feeling like a failure or a slacker. The other part of being an independent forty-something woman who has to regain her footing in life is being willing to do what's necessary to fulfill obligations and stay reasonably sane in the process. Like everyone, I had bills and life responsibilities that didn't really care about my $6,500 financial loss in an internet phishing scam or about my two graduate degrees.

I had to hustle, and Uber was hiring. I took many side gigs while I got back to myself. I had a crisis in confidence along the way, and struggled many days to make meaning out of losing as much as I had all at once, but I just kept believing that things would work themselves out. And when I couldn't believe it, my best friend reminded me. I knew from life experience that when everything seems to go to hell at the same time, the universe is definitely trying to get your attention. I was listening.

I knew that I had been out of alignment for several years, both in my career and in my romantic relationship, but I didn't know how to fix any of it or what I might need. Fear showed up as indecision and self-doubt for those years until God helped me out, right out of a "good job" and out of a relationship with a man I really wanted to work things out with. But I had outgrown those things in those forms. I felt it. I knew it. Still, living it was one of the hardest things I've ever had to work through. My ego learned to take a backseat, and I learned to value myself just as I was. Many of the new people I was meeting didn't even know about the letters after my name or fancy Hollywood life I had been living. They didn't know that I was Dr. Darnise, that I was coaching famous women when I wasn't driving people around in my car. We were just people from varying walks of life trying to make a living. Those experiences felt bad sometimes, but they helped me put myself back together again like the prodigal daughter who forgot who she was and where home was. As I began to remember, the phone began to ring and doors of opportunity began to open.

I was asked to come back to the school in a staff position initially to replace my former colleague who was out on disability leave. I was scheduled to be there for two months . . . and then another month . . . and then he decided not to return to his job. Then I was offered classes to teach. Of course at this point I had to step back and say, "Wait. What's going on here? Things are starting to look a lot like they used to. What's up with this?" I had been leaning a lot on my spirituality during these difficult times, so it was normal for me to have prayerful conversation with my angels, and they reminded me of something I already knew: when you want to know if you've really grown or made inner changes, don't look at the outer circumstances to gauge it. Watch your own inner reactions when the same people or situations show up again, because they most likely will. If your response is different, then you've made a change;

if your response is the same as it has always been, meaning that fear, doubt, and ego still take you out over the same situations, then you have not grown.

As my career landscape started to populate itself again, I continued to remind myself, "I don't want a full-time job. I'm not an employee; I am an independent contractor and entrepreneur. I have clients to serve, books to write, choices to make, and I will keep my priorities in order this time." That was my guiding motto as I watched my world repopulate itself with goodies from the past and the introduction of some new gifts. It was important to me to stay in alignment with my truest self. I could now trust that everything would work out for the best, and the most important thing for me was to remember to design my life around who I really am, rather than, as most of us learn to do, create a life around a job and eke out a life in the margins. I had already been down that road, and I was not about to take that trip again.

I teach my clients to lean into the direction of their goals and dreams. You have to begin where you are to create a life you love. I know that it can be done, and that it works because of my own experiences. Set your sights on where you want to go, how you most want to live your life, and watch universal magic happen that will align the details for you in ways that you cannot imagine.

Radical Lesson #5

Be Authentic in All Aspects of Your Life

"Who are you, and what do you want for your life at this time?"

My coaching sessions with new clients begin with self-identity. Without a clear sense of self we proceed in vain. Knowing and loving yourself are the foundations upon which we begin to build fruitful lives or course correct those that need it. I'm not interested in professional titles or accomplishments when I ask this question. I am interested in how a woman understands herself without external labels or validations. Who are you at your core without your mask of respectability? Most people cannot answer this question quickly or easily. I don't expect them to. I'm hoping you will begin working with this question now as you continue reading this book. Don't be too quick to answer it—sit with the question for a while, and see what truth comes up.

When things fall apart in your life, particularly when everything in your life seems to fall apart at the same time, you are having a very intense, advanced, master class in spiritual growth. You are learning at an accelerated rate that what's real is on the

---

40 Something Nugget of Wisdom

Living authentically takes courage and the ability to resist outside forces that want you to hide your true self.

---

inside, and what's on the outside is only temporary and inconsistent. One cannot base one's life, livelihood, or self-worth on any exterior thing or person. This simple truth is the foundation for everyone on a spiritual path, and that means all of us.

We are constantly bombarded with the marketing of products we're supposed to use to create externally based self-images. We are all told we need that new car, the bigger house, the better wardrobe, the fancier school, and VIP status everywhere we go in order to be successful and happy. We are told these are the things that will give us everything we want, and most of us believe it. It is generally only when we have a life-crushing experience that we begin to understand the delusion we have all been living under.

It would be one thing if we all had a good understanding of self and then added on the luxury items as the accessories and toys that they were meant to be, but in reality what has happened is that we have substituted these things for the authentic self-worth and well-being that we really need and want. Then, when these things do go away for whatever reason—job loss, divorce, repossession, foreclosure, bankruptcy—many of us are left with an identity problem, leaving us feeling vulnerable, exposed, and simply scared to death. We have no idea who we are apart from these things. We become too intimidated to even accept social invitations because we don't know how to answer the question, "So, what do *you* do?" We feel inadequate, like failures. Many people begin to isolate themselves and fall into depression because they have no idea who they really are.

What if you could be yourself?

The first three questions I ask my clients to answer are: Who am I? What do I want now? What will it cost me if I don't make a change? As simple as these questions seem, the answers are generally not so easily accessible. Try answering them for yourself. What do you come up with? Most of us have buried these things for so long that it takes time to excavate them, reclaim them, and then start to live them. Trust the answers that bubble up, and believe that the things you want are possible.

Authenticity in Relationships

Over the years I've learned a lot about relationships and about human behavior in general. Relationship work is the primary focus with my clients because so many people struggle in this area. Everyone wants to be loved and accepted, but most of us have trouble working that out with another person. I work with clients to unpack a lot of the emotional baggage they are carrying to clear the way for fulfilling and loving partnerships. This requires a lot of truth-telling, forgiveness work, and willingness to let things go.

My relationships have taught me about being emotionally available, letting down my guard, and incorporating someone else into my life plans. While it is true that I have always had a lot of suitors, I have not often had deeply connected relationships. I found it much easier to keep a few men on rotation, maintaining a platonic dating situation for a while, maybe choosing one for the friend with benefits role, and eventually hitting the reset button on all of them to start over by myself and eventually with a fresh, new crew. This plan allowed me to stay emotionally distant and safe, and stay on track in my career. It worked well for me. I had no time to stop for a man. If he wanted to run with me for a while, great; if he wanted to be too serious or—gasp—get married, I became the runaway bride. I couldn't for the life of me figure out why so many women were so desperate to find a man and settle down. That sounded like stagnation and boredom to me. So I kept it moving.

The closer and more intimate the relationship, the more opportunity for self-discovery. I say "opportunity" because many do not take the trip down the path to growth when something goes wrong in a relationship. Most people just blame the other person and continue with the dysfunction they have become used to. Growth still happens in baby steps. God does not give up on us, but we could have more quantum leaps if we could tolerate the turbulence that they will create. Intimate partners get to see us in ways that no one else does. They see us when the civil behavior is set aside. They see us when we are in pain, angry, and vulnerable. In other relationships we can cover these things up. We can even hide from ourselves with busywork and addictive behaviors, but our partners see us, and they are close enough to touch those issues we have learned to keep away from everyone else. We always have the choice to take the opportunity for growth that the relationship offers or to settle in for the comfortable ride with someone who doesn't cause us to feel quite so deeply.

Another gift of being a healthy forty-something is that we grow past romanticizing every date we have. Maybe you remember the fantasy of trying on every date's last name, imagining the wedding, even the kids' names? Maybe in your thirties you felt anxious about not being married or even coupled up, so you dated guys with potential who you wanted to change into your dream man? These kinds of episodes plague so many of us, but then you get to forty-something and see more wisely that you don't need to do any of that. No more chasing, no more fixer-upper projects, no more waiting for that call or text. You may still long for marriage and family, but the advantage of life experience has taught you not to pursue dead-end relationships, and not to invest your best self in someone who doesn't reciprocate.

Experience has taught you your value such that you are discerning about the person with whom you share your time and bed. You know now that a fling or a one-night stand, should you choose to have one, is just that. You can keep a level head and not turn that man into your husband. You have learned the answer to the younger woman's pained question, "Why doesn't he call me?" You know that love is a verb, and that you don't have to convince someone who really loves you. You know how to get on with your life when one man turns out to be a dud. Even if you have to lick your wounds after a failed relationship or series of bad dates, you know that you will survive. If you are honest with yourself, you know the signs when something is real or when it's not. You can trust your own intuitive voice that whispers to you on the inside, "Not this one," and have the courage to walk away. Your experience gives you perspective that you didn't have before. You can rejoice when your heart recognizes that you are talking to an authentic, honest man. The forties offer a radical opportunity for self-discovery and awakening.

Back to my story about my relationship with Bill. That borrowed time from Christmas Day was up! Our relationship was pretty much over, but we were living that Gladys Knight song: neither one of us wanted to be the first to say good-bye. Ugh! It was just awful. What was I to do? How could I be a relationship coach without a relationship? But how long was I willing to go along in an unfulfilling relationship that was turning sour?

It was something of a puzzle how we had managed to remain together for as long as we had. The first three years had been a serious roller coaster of emotions for both of us. We were both used to being the one who was pursued in relationships. Neither of us was used to being the pursuer. Being pursued and being a pursuer are two different energies. Both of us considered ourselves to be the prize. We continually misunderstood each other. We continually felt offended, slighted, and generally unsupported by the other. We took everything personally. We sought guidance from professionals, and that seemed to help for a while, but we still had problems. What kept us going was that we were able to have really good times together, too.

We definitely enjoyed each other's company. We had our designated mid-week date night and honored Sundays as days for just ourselves. We spent a lot of time together one-on-one. A lot of this time was actually good. But somehow, in some way, something would happen, and we would have a major—and I do mean major—blowup. It would be the kind of meltdown that would make me want to run for the hills and wonder why I bothered. I would tell my friends that I could just as easily be a cat lady and be happy. I did not need that man making me crazy. But it was those happier times that gave us hope that there must be some reason for us to be together. Still, sometimes I felt I was just in it for the appearance of having a relationship, because the good times became fewer and farther between.

Maybe it was at one of the low points that I realized just how caught up I was with appearances. This went beyond just personal vanity; I was concerned about my public image. I have spent a good deal of my adult life cultivating a very specific image of myself as a professional woman who always has everything all together. I invested a lot of time and energy into presenting myself as being someone who does not have any sort of drama or messy emotions cluttering up her life. Maintaining such an image had of course cost me in the area of relationships before. But I hadn't thought the cost was very great. After all, I could easily find new partners, and having a number of casual relationships really felt alright with me. I did not perceive myself as needing to have very much intimacy with any one person.

Intimacy involves vulnerability, and that was just about the last thing I was trying to engage in with anyone. Most of my relationships existed at arm's-length, and that was good enough for me. I had never really expected to have a deep, intimate relationship with a partner. I had not seen emotionally expressive kinds of relationships modeled in my life, so I did not yearn for one. However, over time, I did come to value feeling nurtured, loved, and supported.

Being in relationship with Bill meant a crash course in developing emotional authenticity. I was not prepared for that. Had I known getting involved with him would mean that, I would've run for the hills and never looked back. Being in relationship with Bill meant that I could not hide from my emotions. I could not hide from my own feelings of vulnerability. I could not hide from the fact that I had been hiding most of my life. Thus, our romantic relationship for me was an exercise in spiritual growth and expansion.

Of course, this is what I teach my clients all the time: relationships are spiritual work. People normally think of relationships as vehicles by which they feel love and can be supportive, romantic, and passionate with a partner who cares for them and has their back. But that is only the tip of the iceberg. The universe uses relationships to help us grow in a multitude of ways. The more we are willing to look at our relationships as reflections of who we are, the more we are able to learn from them spiritually. If we only view relationships as vehicles for romance, marriage, and babies, we miss the larger point. Fortunately, the universe is onto us before we even know what the game is. The universe brings us into interactions with people who are on the same vibrational frequency that we are on, and therefore we really cannot escape ourselves.

Each relationship is a reflection of our authentic selves. Each relationship has the capacity to teach us more about ourselves if we will allow it. If we do not allow it, we will spend our relationships blaming the other person, being angry at the other person, and wanting the other person to change. If we see our relationships as reflections, then we have the opportunity to see the things that need to be healed within us. The clues are the very things that irritate you the most about your partner. Why do those particular things irritate you? Most likely it is not simply a matter of being annoyed because your partner left the cap off of the toothpaste tube; more likely it is that their actions, comments, or beliefs stir up something that is within you already. They didn't bring you that hot button—they found it there. When you realize that, you can begin to reflect and ask yourself, Why is this button here? How long has it been here? What created this button? That is the deep work that relationships inspire within us. Again, it is up to us to choose to delve into that work.

As long as I was not delving deeply into my own spiritual and emotional work, my relationship with Bill would be full of things that only made me feel more angry, unloved, and unsupported. The more I resisted exploring my own emotions, the more things would happen to inspire my emotions to erupt. Of course, none of these "inspiring moments" would be anything that I would consciously choose to engage, because they all seemed very hard and painful. My first inclination was always to run, to leave him. I just could not bear having to deal with such volatile emotions. Emotions to me were messy, irrational, and crazy-making. I much preferred my facade of seeming cool, reserved, and somewhat aloof. However, the longer the relationship continued, the more "inspirational moments" happened. I hated it. I resisted and ran away many times.

Eventually, I began to have an awareness that what I was really running away from was being vulnerable, being authentic, being able to ask for what I wanted. Those were my hot button issues, and he definitely found them. When he brushed up against them, I felt exposed, vulnerable, and emotionally unsafe because I was so unused to dealing with emotions at all. I felt I couldn't bear it.

Right in there was where my emotional, psychological, and spiritual work needed to happen. Right there in that narrow crevice is where I needed to go to have healing that would allow me to experience real connection, support, and love with someone else. I always teach that the universe is very precise, and it certainly was for me. I was faced with exactly the wound that needed attention and healing. Many times, my clients have said to me over the years, "But why do I have to work on this thing? It is the hardest thing for me." Or they would say, "Why is it always this?" And I would say, "Because it is *your* thing, and the universe knows it, and you know it too. Consider this situation an opportunity for your growth and well-being. If you don't take it as that, and learn from it and grow now, scenarios like this will only repeat themselves in your life. If you are unwilling to face it, the situations will only get bigger and more serious. At some point you will no longer be able to avoid dealing with them." Yes, I was indeed speaking to myself.

And then came the day that I finally faced the full unvarnished truth about my relationship with Bill. It had to end. I was clear about that. It was true. We were not partners building something together. We weren't on the same page—we weren't even in the same book. Instead, we were just keeping each other company, and not very good company at that. I had the revelation that I must tell the absolute truth, even if only to myself. I decided to tell my best friend, as if she didn't already know. Best friends always know! The ball was set in motion, and the universe was conspiring with my decision.

After another round of arguments with Bill had led to me sleeping on his couch, I had a moment of clarity that caused me to chuckle to myself, "Oh I see what you are doing, God. You are helping me to see things so clearly that I cannot possibly stay here. All of this crazy is for me to see it and get it." Early the next morning, Bill woke me up and told me he was leaving for the gym, and that I could move to the bed if I wanted to. I did, but a couple of hours later, I awoke with a start and heard a very clear intuitive voice, "Get up and leave this house right now!" Immediately, my feet hit the floor; I went to the bathroom, put on my clothes, took a look around for anything I had to have, and left quickly. As I was leaving, Bill drove up—he was coming home early. I waved and didn't look back. I knew that I could not go back. Otherwise, I would become like Lot's wife in the Bible, turned to a pillar of salt as she looked back at her former life. I knew I had to move forward.

I was shaking with adrenaline and feeling as if I would have an anxiety attack, but I drove myself home knowing that once again I had divine guidance to keep me on track. I had gotten completely out of alignment with myself. In full people-pleasing mode, I had sacrificed my own entrepreneurial goals—not because Bill demanded it, but because I thought the relationship needed it, and that he would be happier if I did. In this situation, people pleasing had been a colossal disaster! But what I would eventually come to understand is that it needed to be a disaster. I needed the clarity that came with the Bill experience. In a metaphysical sense, I sent myself that experience. I needed the reminder to be true to myself, tell my own truth, and not sacrifice what was dearest to me. Doing so would always end badly. My angels told me quite clearly, "This is not permitted. Any attempts you make to dim your own light to satisfy another or give away your power will lead to unhappiness and extreme dis-ease." I was clear that my lesson was to stand up on my own two feet, live my life with authenticity and even vulnerability, and move faithfully toward my own light. Therein lies my success. I was starting to catch a truer vision of myself, but I had more to learn.

What happens when it is time or even past time for a relationship to end, but you stay anyway? The truth is that by staying past the expiration date on that relationship you sell yourself out. The details will vary in each woman's story, but, in truth, our own inner voice tells us, "Now is the time to go," and fear and insecurity rear their heads, and we say, "but I can't."

I certainly knew before the fourth and final year of my relationship with Bill that things were unlikely to shift in our favor, and when I finally made the break, I was relieved, but grieving. I was not interested in dating anyone for a good long while, and when I first ventured back into the dating pool, the men who began to show up in my life reflected exactly where I was: unavailable and sporadic in temperament and behavior. One man did have my attention to some degree, however.

Ray was a successful businessman who liked the finer things in life, much as I do, and we began going out occasionally. Each time, Ray would name-drop an expensive Beverly Hills restaurant, and we would go. He would spend most of his time talking about himself, his business goals, and his vision to get married. He had decided that I was to be his wife, and that I could help him with his business. He had a few ideas for me as well, but primarily he needed my assistance to help him find a new house, secure his new car, and research office space for his expanding business. Sometimes he would hand me money: "Here, sweetie, this is for you." It would be $200 to $300 at a time. "What's this for?" I would ask. "I just figured you need it," he would say.

That seemed fine at first. But wait! Nothing was fine at all. Here was a man many women dream of—successful, generous, marriage-minded. But, on closer inspection, I had to ask myself, What exactly is playing out here? Is this man generally interested in what I have planned for myself and my future, or is he expecting that my interests will be secondary to his already successful business? Was he someone with whom I felt comfortable, could easily talk to, and could imagine building a life with? Was he interested in a wife who was a whole person, or was he interested in finding someone to fill a role in his world? I continued to see Ray with these questions foremost in my mind. There were some aspects that I found interesting and fun about him, but I always came back to his actual behavior and words. I stepped back from it all to really have a look. Here is what I finally told myself: "You are dangerously close to selling yourself out to a man and relationship that simply looks good on the outside. You have walked this path before in a relationship where you lost your identity and sidelined your own work. Are you willing to do that again for material comforts? You could surely have many luxuries, but you would only be able to fit your real self in around the edges of his world. Are you going to do that again?"

Ouch, this was the real truth! I knew it was a replay of where I had been with Bill: different face, very similar scenario. Then a funny thing happened. I began to think of other women I could set Ray up with. I kept thinking there must be someone I know who is looking for just this type of arrangement. She would be happy to apply her skills and knowledge to helping her rich husband's business thrive. I never did think of anyone, but I declined to go on any more dates with Ray. My vision was getting clearer and continuing to pull me into alignment with myself. The angel on my shoulder had just made it plain for me, and I knew I would not sell myself out for thirty pieces of silver. I expected better for myself. I've said it before: our outer circumstances don't change first, so our inner attitude and behavior must change first.

When that old scenario shows up again, and it will, will you behave differently? Will you make a new, empowered choice from where you now stand? That is the mark of authentic change.

The Real Me, the Real You

Life is generally messy for people at some point. People need to know that their leaders and teachers understand that about life. This is what makes a teacher a valuable resource to a student. When I began to develop my coaching business, I realized that women could benefit from knowing that I sometimes had self-doubt, vulnerability issues, problems in my relationships, and financial worries. These are typical life challenges, and the women I could help needed to know that I know what they have been going through. Before I came to that realization, I thought that people would only want to pay for someone's professional advice if that person was herself one-hundred percent together. However, my own life was showing me something different.

I watched other women who were business leaders, entrepreneurs, professors, and celebrities; I saw them in their glory, commanding audiences, receiving praise, publishing books, receiving large paychecks. I thought, But how did they get there? I was fortunate enough to be close up to many successful women. I was in some pretty exclusive company—VIP rooms, red carpets, and fabulous homes and board rooms. Many times I would think to myself, "I know that this successful businesswoman is standing before me telling me about how she built her business from nothing, working from her kitchen table with her cat on her lap and living off of ramen noodles, but all I see right now is a successful, well-dressed, attractive, wealthy woman. What I really want to know, girlfriend, is how did you get there given the vicissitudes of life? What did you do when things were really tough? Did you have self-doubt? Whom did you turn to when you felt that you were at your wits' end? How did you muster up the courage on a daily basis to keep going when it seemed the reasonable thing to do was to get a nine-to-five office job? What did you tell yourself when your dragon showed up, breathing fire and scaring you to death? What is your best advice for continuing to put one foot in front of the other and making a way out of no way?"

Funny how I wanted to know those things about other women. I yearned to know their answers to those questions. However, it did not dawn on me in the initial phases of building my coaching business that women would want to know the truth about me and the challenges I'd faced, so that they could connect with me as a real person. It took me several years to appreciate the value of sharing my own story fully and authentically. I finally learned that my business success comes from making a real, heartfelt connection with others using my story—my vulnerabilities, transitions, crossroads, confusion, fear, and reinvention.

Dina's Story

Dina was thirty-eight, and felt depressed and at loose ends about the direction her life was taking. She wondered how she was ever going to "get to happy by forty." Her confusion and angst led her to hire me as her coach. Dina told me that she had been a bright star in her family; she was successful at school, and her parents were proud of her. After earning a degree in finance from Georgetown University, she decided to go to law school—with her parents' blessing. She worked and traveled for about two years and was accepted into the University of Southern California Law School, which is a pretty big deal.

Dina moved to Los Angeles, began classes, and soon after began to hate it. But she didn't admit that truth to anyone. She simply worked harder, determined to make herself like it. The other truth that Dina had never shared with anyone in her family was that she was a lesbian. She felt that she could never admit this because then everyone would be disappointed. She continually felt like a failure because she couldn't be true to herself. Eventually Dina dropped out of law school, which she said was necessary for her survival: "There is no way that I wanted that life. It would have eaten me up."

She remained in L.A., got a job, and began dating women. With her family in Maryland she could keep up a dual life. It got easier over the years to play a role during short visits home. She felt that her father was already greatly disappointed because she had left law school. He continued to nudge her into going back. She managed to side-step the issue. Her family often asked if she was dating anyone, and by "anyone" they meant a man who might be good enough to marry and have children with. Dina side-stepped this issue too.

Then two years passed without Dina returning home for the holidays. Her mother was worried; she and Dina's father wanted to visit her in California. Dina realized the time had come to tell the truth. She had to find a way to tell her family and not come apart in the process. She was now forty, and wanted to "just be happy finally." My advice to her was this: "Prioritize yourself, and tell your truth. You cannot know how others will respond to you, but life feels burdensome and depressing when you can't be yourself. Remember that you deserve to be happy; you do not have to sacrifice that for anyone else. Make choices that align with your highest truth, and it will always work out, even though it may not be easy." We worked together to identify her actual goals and life vision. She had almost lost track from playing so many roles her whole life.

As it turned out, Dina wanted to go to school for counseling, so she began applying to graduate programs. She said that her father would not think very highly of this decision, but she knew it was right for her. She had come around to feeling that her forties would be her own. In the end, her parents reluctantly admitted that they knew she hadn't been completely honest with them in the past. They had begun to worry that she had fallen into "weird" company in Hollywood. Dina reported to me that after she came out to them as lesbian, after she got the words out of her mouth, she immediately felt as if the weight of the world had been lifted from her shoulders. For the first time she felt happy.

Her parents didn't quite understand her "lifestyle," but they were trying, and they didn't reject her, which she had always feared. This new sense of relief and joy also allowed her to have better relationships. Because she wasn't hiding, because she was being authentic, she could be a better partner, and she could go beyond casually dating. Dina had a lot to sort out "to get to happy," but I reassured her that forty-something would turn out to be great.

Show the World Your Authentic Self

Do you have the courage to let the world see your power and your beauty? Can you be bold enough to use all of your gifts? I call it "using everything your mama gave you." If you are brilliant and beautiful, let it be known. If you've been holding back on being the smartest person in the room, that's over! If you are a great leader but have been too afraid to show it because someone may call you a bitch, later for that. My understanding of the word "bitch" is this: it is another person's pathetic response to the fact that a woman is not going along with their plan for her. You can reject this and claim your own gifts and power. Besides, sticks and stones . . .

You've got a mission to accomplish! The most radical thing about the decade of the forties is that you can finally answer your inner calling, which is now at the highest it has been since your childhood, when you learned to diminish your natural light. This is the time of your transformation if you will allow it. With your forties comes the blessed dissatisfaction with the status quo of over-giving and being insecure, hiding in the shadows of your own glory. It is this dissatisfaction that comes from the pain and limitations of living a shadow life. You have the opportunity and the courage to create the life you really want to live. That is my definition of authenticity.

Who does your authentic self call you to be? What will it cost you if you don't answer?

Radical Lesson #6

Learn from the Patterns in Your Life

We are all destined to behave according to the patterns we learned as children, for better or worse. If we remain unconscious, without personal reflection and insight, we will act according to the coping mechanisms that we formed as children. Insofar as we remain unconscious, we are on autopilot, puzzled as to why our situations never work out the way we want. We remain in frustrating relationships of all kinds. We unconsciously reenact our patterns with new people and in new situations, hoping and expecting for a different outcome.

For example, some people are always on edge, expecting a hostile, antagonistic environment. If you are one of these people, you are always ready for a fight whether it be with a waiter, a bank teller, a coworker, or a mate. You might perceive that "they are trying to get one over on me," leading you to feel the need to defend yourself, perhaps verbally or even physically attacking another person. You

---

40 Something Nugget of Wisdom

Ask yourself: What's the source of this unhealthy pattern? Why does it keep happening in my life? What wounds do I need to heal in order to break the pattern?

---

may have grown up in an environment that was hostile, neglectful, or abusive, so you did not get your emotional needs met. As a result, you remain ready to force people to treat you right. What you are not conscious of is that when this is a reoccurring circumstance, you are the common denominator, and you are the one bringing that energy into every setting that you walk into.

As hard as it may be to hear, it's not them; it's you. It is all of us when we are acting unconsciously. The good news is that these old wounds can be healed if they are first acknowledged for what they are—the child still trying to get love and attention—and then processed in more healthy and productive ways. However, if you refuse to see your patterns and own the drama you are continually acting out, the cycle will continue, and you will lead a life of hostility, anger, and bitterness, because it will never lead to the wholeness you really desire. Sister friend, I have to tell you, "Girl, just let your guard down; not everything is a fight. You must be tired." The emotional pain is not punishment; it is a call to action and growth. Pain is a reminder that an old wound needs tending and care. Otherwise it will fester and poison your entire life.

Using the Enneagram to Recognize Your Patterns

The enneagram is one type of system that helps us recognize the patterns that we are living out, whether in work, friendships, or love. I use the enneagram in my coaching work to facilitate such healing. It is a personality system based on nine types, similar to zodiac signs, which designate us with a number that corresponds to our childhood experiences and how we developed in response to them. These responses and behaviors remain with us throughout our lives, even if, as some researchers suggest, we shift slightly from one number to another over time. When we are aware and conscious, we operate at a high-functioning aspect of our number. When we are unaware, asleep at the wheel of our own lives, or experiencing stress or trauma, we operate at a low-functioning aspect of our respective number. There many books and resources available on the topic; I particularly recommend publications by Helen Palmer and Don Riso.

In more self-disclosure here, I am a three, the "Overachiever/Workaholic" in the enneagram system. I have been in the company of people who eagerly share their numbers with others as banter and cocktail conversation, which is their choice; however, I always wonder if people realize that they are giving away a lot of information about themselves, including their deepest emotional wounding. These numbers represent aspects of ourselves that we use to find our way in the world even when we do not feel okay about ourselves. They reveal how we experienced childhood and how we learned to behave in order to function within our family units and in society. In a way, we are giving people access to our soft underbellies, where we are most vulnerable.

I took on the characteristics of an overachiever somewhere along the way in childhood because I had a mother who was very demanding, not very emotionally nurturing, but who always looked for the best in me through my achievements, which meant excellent school performance and good-girl behavior. My mom didn't reward me with statements of love or encouraging talks and pats on the back; instead, she scrutinized my grades and behavior. When those things were good, then I was good, and I felt her approval. When she thought I should do better, then I was not good, and I felt her disapproval. That's easy math even for a child who struggled and literally cried trying to do math homework. I learned to do what I needed to do to get her approval and positive attention. I performed according to her expectations, and that was the life I knew. I likewise felt this type of pressure from other members of my family, so I had even more reason to keep it up. I was rewarded with good grades and adult approval. Great! What could be the problem here?

The problem with a personality type that seeks outward approval in order to feel good is that it is not sustainable. Your self-worth cannot be determined by outer circumstances or other people. That inner work has to be done, and life will help you out with hard lessons until you gain some consciousness about who you are. In many stressful situations in my life, I have retreated into my work. While I enjoy my work, I feel as if I have about ten jobs or commitments at any given time, and I am prone to be severely out of balance in terms of my work and my personal life. I can lose myself in work for weeks or even months at a time before I tap out in exhaustion. I am no stranger to burnout. It is hard for me to relate to people who seem to have no stamina or discipline for getting things done. I admit that I judge people harshly who seem to get by without putting in hard work. And I'm super mad if I put in a lot of work and I don't get at least basic recognition for my efforts. It's an equation that I worked out years ago, and it is always supposed to end with me getting at least a thank you if not exuberant fanfare (just kidding). I continually have to check myself with such judgments. Other people don't have to and don't need or want to work the way I do, and they are perfectly good people. When I lose my balance, I have to catch myself and ask, "Who am I performing for now? What's going on in my life that has triggered this old patterned response?"

Rita's Story

One of the top relationship issues I hear from women is meeting undesirable men, and meeting them over and over again. I call them Repeat Performances. I want to share with you one client's story as a way of seeing how our programming affects our choices.

Rita likes younger men, usually in the range of twenty-five to thirty-five years old. Rita also is very nice and nurturing and loves to help people. She's the kind of friend who goes the extra mile, gives her last dollar to help, and opens up her home. She is a great friend to have.

Rita's pattern is that she meets a young guy and becomes smitten because he's very cute, funny, and charming, but then she discovers the poor guy doesn't have much going on professionally or financially. He might be broke or between jobs or whatever. What do you think Rita does? If you guessed "take him in and take care of him," you're right.

Now she does this out of the goodness of her heart and figures it will just be for a short time to help the guy get on his feet. When he does, he'll be the perfect partner, because then he'll be financially stable and able to take care of her.

Does this ever happen? No. Does she see it coming from one guy to the next? No. Each guy has his own story and scenario, so it seems different to her.

Now you might be saying, "Well, that's dumb. I would never end up in a situation like that." But really? Think about the situations you have ended up in. Would you have ever predicted it? I'm not at all trying to be judgmental, just pointing out that we all have our blind spots and repeatedly fall for the same person in different clothing. It just might be a different set of particulars for you.

Well, to wrap up Rita's story: We were working together and one day she said, "I met a guy—he's cute, and yes, he's young. But he asked me out, and I was excited to be asked out, so I said yes. It didn't seem like a big deal because we were just going to get a quick bite to eat at a café, right then after our class. So, we go, we eat, we have a decent conversation. Then, the bill comes. He's got no money and doesn't even attempt an explanation for not paying. No conversation about going Dutch. Nothing."

She paid it because she's nice and didn't want to embarrass him. They exchanged good-byes.

When she told me this story, I said, "Hmmm. Does he remind you of anyone?"

The light came on, and she said, "Oh my God. He's just like the others!"

And I said, "What are you going to do when you see him in class again, or he calls and asks you out?"

She thought about it and then said, "Well, it's going to be hard, because he's cute, and I did kind of like him, but I'm going to say no."

"What is the truth that you need to know about yourself in attracting this kind of relationship?"

"It's hard to look at, but I think I'm coming from a place of taking care of others to prove myself worthy. I've been trying to get love by over-giving, hoping someone will love me back for that, because it has seemed to me that no one would love me completely just for me. So I find the guy who needs help over and over again."

So now she could begin to break her pattern.

I also helped her create a specific plan to find more appropriate men. After that, she clearly saw the old dating pattern and could make a better choice in line with what she really wanted. Repeating that pattern was a waste of time and would not lead her where she wanted to be. She would just continue to be disappointed, resentful, and out of more money misspent on yet another guy.

Know Your Relationship Patterns

So do you see how if you are not aware, and no one helps you become aware, you might fall into the same patterns, and actually keep yourself away from the committed, responsible person you actually want to be with?

In plain talk, if you are a jealous person, it means that you are insecure. Figure out what led to this insecurity. Don't point a finger at the partners in your life. Dig deeper and get to the source. What happened in your life that left you feeling crushed and emotionally needy, yet distrustful? If you have trust issues, it means that your defense mechanisms are in overdrive, and you may come across as suspicious, unavailable, and interrogating. Testing other people to see if they are worthy is just not fair. They will almost always fail your tests anyway because, frankly, you need to learn that your insecurity needs some attention and healing. The pain you feel each time someone fails one of your tests is an indicator for you to turn within and get some healing. Otherwise, love can't get through your walls. What is the earliest time in your life when you can remember putting your walls up?

If you ignore big red flags about your partner or blame another woman or man for your relationship problems, you are afraid and not acting out of integrity. You are not telling the truth, and you are resistant to the truth revealing itself to you. Don't blame the relationship you're in or the one you just got out of; put on your big girl panties, and do your spiritual work. Why are you in a relationship with someone who disrespects you? Why do you feel unlovable or like you have to fight to keep someone in your life? Who was the first person who broke your heart in that way? This is the work.

I imagine that you may say, "But wait, it's true that the people I date are often liars or that they cheat. I'm suspicious because all I meet are these kinds of people. Is something wrong with me, or is something wrong with them?" My response to that, because I hear it a lot, is this: you are the common denominator in your life and relationships. You cannot attract something into your experience unless you are of like energy or have agreed to participate. The pain and low self-worth that you feel and carry around is a beacon for additional experiences that match that feeling, no matter how many affirmations you say.

Vibration overrides words. You will repeat patterns that reinforce your dominant feelings and beliefs. If you believe all men cheat, then you will attract cheating men. On the other hand, this does not have to be your experience. You can also acknowledge that, indeed, some men do cheat, but that it is not something that is part of your personal life. You decide and design a life focused on the character traits that you actually want, with no energy given to traits that you do not want.

Here it may get a little tricky for some people because they think that by listing what they don't want, they are listing what they do want. For example, you might say, "I love the idea of having an honest, faithful man in my life." This is a very different energy than saying, "I don't want a man who cheats." Can you feel the difference? The former is focused on the desirable traits, and the latter is focused on the undesirable traits. Clarify what you mean and how you are actually talking to yourself. There need be no mystery here: your life experiences reflect your beliefs and daily self-talk. In what ways are these experiences good for you, and in what ways are they not good for you? What type of people and encounters do you regularly have? They are your instructors.

A higher level of spiritual teaching around this concept is to ask yourself, "Why would I have sent myself this experience? In all the world of people and situations I could be having, why these? How do they have the potential to benefit me?" The advanced spiritual student recognizes their own power and responsibility for their own life. Blaming other people or circumstances is limited thinking. Step back from your pain and circumstance enough to get perspective. This is why doing the inner work of uncovering and healing is essential to your well-being and your healthy relationships.

How do you make your relationship choices? How do you decide if you are going to share yourself with a particular person? Do you set standards for yourself or for the person you're dating? I know many of us like to say we have standards, but when it comes down to feeling lonely one time too many or going with Mr. or Ms. Right Now, sometimes we make disempowered, very poor decisions that repeatedly lead to heartbreak. How many Repeat Performances have you had in your life—different face, same scenario? By this decade, you likely have had enough life experiences to recognize your own pattern. Now, as a more grounded, centered, and self-assured forty-something, you should be much clearer about what you want, what you don't want, and how you will spend your time. With that kind of clarity, staying away from partners who are not a match and choosing partners who are becomes easier. As you appreciate your own value and worth more, you expect others to appreciate you as well.

Radical Lesson #7

Set Healthy Boundaries

"No" is a complete sentence. However, for many of us it is difficult to respond to a request with a firm no. As women we have been groomed to be nice, sweet, and accommodating, which means we feel we can never say no to a request for help or a favor. If we do, we risk being considered selfish, mean, bitchy, not a team player, and then we'll feel bad about ourselves, as if we have failed at being a good and nice person. While it is challenging, I have noticed that with an increasing sense of self-worth, it becomes easier to give an unequivocal no to someone's request without feeling like a terrible person. If for no other reason, by our forties we have exhausted ourselves doing things for other people, and even though many times we want to be helpful and available, a lot of times we end up doing things out of a sense of obligation, which leads us into resentment.

After running ourselves into this wall throughout our lives, many of us come to the point where we say, "Enough already. No, I cannot babysit your kids. No, I cannot host your baby shower. No, I cannot take on extra work without being compensated. No, I cannot drive you around doing your errands with you." And, if for

---

40 Something Nugget of Wisdom
Maintaining strong boundaries is a direct reflection of how much you value your own time and well-being.

---

no other reason than exhaustion and resentment, we can say no without making up an excuse. My reason for not driving someone to the airport is not, "No. I have a doctor's appointment," instead it's "No, I'm sorry. I'm not available." If they're really in a bind, I might offer my Uber account; otherwise, I am not available to drive them at 6:00 in the morning. (I'll be sleeping, and would rather do anything else!) The problem with giving an excuse, "I can't because . . ." is that people will work around your excuse to get their own needs met. They'll say, "Okay, but how about picking me up from the airport when I get back?" Or, "how about watching my dog at your house while I'm away? He has to be walked every day and has a vet appointment and needs his meds, but he's no trouble." Without boundaries, you will cave, and be in service to your friend *and* her dog!

Maintaining strong boundaries is a direct reflection of how much you value your own time and well-being. Setting your own standards for what is acceptable or loving behavior toward you is an act of self-love; it is not about being mean, rude, or judgmental toward someone else. Do you have your own set of standards in place, or do you allow other people to run their own agenda in your life? Do you know deep down that others take advantage of you? Now is your decade, your time in owning yourself and your full worth. Protect your well-being, and use your energy for the things that matter most to you. You do not owe anyone else your happiness and contentment helping them get to theirs.

Betty's Story

We can see a different way in which someone doesn't set or honor appropriate boundaries in this example from my client Betty.

Betty was a single mother of two boys, aged ten and thirteen at the time. She had a lot of responsibility at her job as a retail manager within a department store. Between her job and managing her household of active boys, Betty had no time for her own self-care. She was exhausted and on autopilot much of the time. She stopped dating because she wanted to focus on raising her kids, and oh, yes, because men just become extra work as well. She didn't have time to add taking care of a man to her life.

I asked her about her belief system that tells her she has to "take care" of a man. She shared her story that in every relationship with a man, she's ended up in the role of managing him and his life. She organized everything: their dates, how they spent their weekends and holidays. She picked his clothes, advised him on healthier things to eat, and told him how to drive.

Me: So you're the boss of the men you are with?
Betty: I'm not trying to be the boss of them, but it always happens.
Me: What is their response, usually?
Betty: They end up hating it, and calling me bossy and controlling. Somehow, I just fall into that role. I know that I'm treating him like he's one of my sons, but I think if I don't, things won't get done.
Me: So what if they don't, or at least not how you would do it?
Betty: Then I would be upset, and feel like I had to fix things or do it over, depending on what it is.
Me: What is the truth you need to know about yourself here?
Betty: That I really am bossy and controlling, I guess.
Me: This is kind of simple really. Just stop doing those things and let him, as a grown man, make his own decisions. Can you be flexible enough to flow his way sometimes, according to the plans he has made?
Betty: I don't think I even know how to step back like that because my life is spent taking care of people or giving them directions on how to do something. It's my autopilot.
Me: Exactly! It is autopilot, but now that you are conscious of it and how it runs your life, you can begin to get perspective.

Set boundaries for yourself that you will not cross, set standards for the men you date, and let them work out their own details. Start with self-observation: see yourself from a slight distance, and pause long enough to make a different decision and action when a situation comes up that you would normally want to take charge of. Count to five, and then ask yourself in the moment before you give a direction, "Why am I telling this adult man how to live his life? What part of me is being served when I do this?"

BETTY: That sounds good, but I know I'm always quick to tell someone how to do something.

ME: Exactly the reason to learn to be self-observant. It is a new skill for you, because you would like to have a new outcome. If you want your life to change, you have to start by changing your life. You're bossy and controlling for a reason, but if you spend time in self-reflection, you will discover why, if you don't already consciously know. Once you know, you disconnect from the power it has over you. *You* begin to make your decisions, not that aspect of you that is in overdrive. Would you say that being bossy has been good for your romantic relationships?

BETTY: Not at all. They don't appreciate it, and truthfully, it's exhausting, and then I don't even enjoy the relationship. I'm doing things they don't even ask me to do, but then I get resentful because I'm carrying more of a load, I feel. It all goes bad after a while, and I guess I've given up on it all. My kids are an excuse for me not to have to be in the dating game. If I'm truthful though, I do actually miss having a man in my life. Unfortunately, I've run off a few of them because I just couldn't stop trying to run their lives. I'm going to work on this.

ME: Yes. I'm going to suggest that you put down those heavy bags of managing everyone, and let yourself be nurtured.

>   Can you set new boundaries knowing that you are actually preserving more of your time and energy, and trust that things will work out? How would that be?
> BETTY: I don't know what to say. . . . That would feel great, but it sounds so foreign to me that I'm going to need to make baby steps.
> ME: We'll walk that road together. First thing is to find out why you have the defense mechanism of needing to control things and people, and then that belief system will begin to fall away. Then you'll start to have different types of relationships. The outer circumstance will reflect your new inner being as you establish better boundaries for yourself and others. Setting boundaries will be good self-care for you too. You're exhausting yourself for no reason.

We did a lot more work together. Betty's resistance came up time and again. Of course, she tried to be the boss of me too, as I expected she would. It's her go-to behavior. We eventually got to a place of honest self-observation. She shared that her home life as a child had been so chaotic and unstable that she vowed to never live like that. She had learned to create a better life for herself by being organized and always planning three steps ahead. This behavior served her well in some cases in her life, but now, as often happens, that same behavior was causing a breakdown in another area of her life. She wasn't even able to have enjoyable romantic relationships as a result of that behavior. The pain of those repeated experiences caused her to seek out my help and to want to recreate what relationships could look like for her.

Boundaries in Relationships

My boundary issue is different from Betty's in terms of my relationships with men. I have mostly dated unavailable men in one form or another. The unavailable man is not just the man who has another woman, but also includes the man who is "too busy" with work, sports, other activities, or simply seems to have no follow-through. When I recall how I had three dates in one day, or how content I was to date a man who was separated but not quite divorced, I have to own that I was in no way, shape, or form ready to commit to anyone's serious relationship.

If you have this problem, here's my advice. Rather than try to get your partner to pay attention to you, or be resentful because you feel you have to compete with everything else in their life, recognize that they have a right to spend their time the way they want to, and in fact they are showing you how they prefer to spend time. As a mature woman, recognize that the person you are dating is simply unavailable, check yourself for your own commitment and vulnerability issues, and move on. Do not spend your time trying to make an unavailable partner become available. It can't be done, unless they decide to do it. Your lesson in the whole affair is to observe and understand the reflection. What is that person showing you about you?

Many of us are walking around with emotional walls or fears that keep us from having the deep, loving relationships we say we want most. Walls will not protect you, but they will, in fact, keep love out. It clicked for me—"Hey, I'm the unavailable one." What needs to click for you? Own that and work to heal it. Your relationships, and your reactions to old relationships, will then begin to shift automatically as a reflection of the new you. As you gain mastery over yourself, when old drama or pesky situations come back into your life, you'll see that your reactions will be different. When that former boyfriend calls, you won't entertain him if you know that you want different things. When someone starts to disrespect you in some way, you will simply leave the environment or firmly set your boundaries.

After my breakup with Bill, I was struggling to reclaim my life. I had become integrated into his household, business, and social life. The separation was visceral and left me feeling defensive and angry. I imagined that this must be what divorce feels like. We were both hurt and angry, and needed time to process the emotional mess that comes from dissolving a four-year relationship. Again, I had to deal with my emotional life, and I was in agony over it. Friends tried to help. They tried to help us get back together, but there was just too much anger on both sides. I also felt that I had lost some of myself. My personal identity was being swallowed up in his, and that was fundamentally untenable for me as a person. I had not been able to manage my authentic being while in a relationship with Bill, so I had to get out. I had to have my own space and breathing room again. Despite our friends' efforts and how much we cared for each other, it was over.

It would be several months before we could even begin to try to be friendly. Before that could happen, I went through a few emotional breakthroughs that mostly resembled bouts of sadness and unexpected tears. They were unexpected because I am usually not an emotionally expressive person, but also because I thought that I had moved past that part. I thought that anger would circumvent heartbreak and lead me directly to recovery. I thought that the hardest part was over, and I could go back to my regularly scheduled life. What I did not anticipate was the layer of emotion that would still be there.

Fortunately, Bill and I were able to get to healing and closure following our breakup. After some time of asking myself why I needed this type of experience, why would I have sent myself this scenario, and how was this good for me, I began to hear the answer: that this was a very good way for me to break open old paradigms of being emotionally distant. What better way, for me anyway, to learn to be open in a relationship than to attract someone who was not open and have to engage him as a reflection of myself? My relationship with him was indeed my spiritual work that leads me now to greater emotional depth and richer relationships.

Bill and I have been able to facilitate this type of healing for each other. The reason we could do so is because we set aside ego enough to become more vulnerable with each other. That which we were unable to do *in* the relationship with each other we were able to do after the breakup. There was no longer any perceived need for pretense or defensiveness or disappointment. We were able to speak very frankly and openly about our feelings and what we had learned about ourselves from each other. We began to have a whole new layer of relationship—not as lovers, but more than just friends. We had finally reached a level of intimacy that had nothing to do with sex. Each of us was willing and able to stand emotionally naked in front of the other and feel accepted and understood. This was remarkable for us. Of course, it would have made all the difference if we had come to this place while we were still in a romantic relationship, but I see that a substantial part of this transformative growth could only happen for me after having gone through the strength-building exercise of breaking up and the resulting self-knowledge.

We are currently sharing what I call Relationship 2.0. It is not what it was romantically, but it is full of a loving affection for each other that has come from healing and new levels of self-understanding. Once the prickly charge of unmet expectations, unspoken needs, and fear of vulnerability could be processed, we were free, and with that freedom came the ability to have a different kind of relationship that seems to fit us. It begins with, and is sustained by, truth-telling.

I'm grateful for the relationship and for the ability to have an open line of communication with him still. It opened me up in brand-new ways, which was just what I needed but didn't recognize. At the end of the forty-something decade, I can see it as a surprising but richly valuable experience. It has taught me how important it is to have emotionally open communications in relationships. It pointed out ways in which I was being inauthentic, still believing that I had to perform in order to be loved. It taught me how to see new potential relationships with greater clarity and how to start telling my truth. Romantic relationships can be our greatest teachers because we pin a unique combination of our hopes, dreams, fantasies, and fears upon them that we don't attach to other types of relationship. No matter how much we project outward upon the other person though, they still point right back to us in the most illuminating ways.

There is another scenario that looms prominently for many women regarding relationships. It is so common, in fact, that I don't have just one example—there are an abundance. Even though many single women long to have a man in their lives, a common mantra that I see and hear is "I don't need a man." Now, usually women who say this are the independent sort, who want it to be known that they are not desperate or needy, and I get that. However, I remind the women I work with that this type of statement and energy is enough to keep men away. Men like to feel needed and appreciated for the things they do for a woman. The woman who is resistant to his assistance and declines it with either her words or her energy will often find herself without a man or the relationship she really wants. In her attempt to establish her own identity and independence, she alienates a man's natural desire to be helpful to the woman he is with.

If this has been your pattern, let down your guard and receive. Feminine energy is receptive and nurturing energy. Allow a man to pour his energy into your being and your life. A man who is a good partner for you will see that you are not needy, but he will want to honor you with his actions and care because he will feel that you deserve it. You will not have to defend your independence. When I found that I was defending myself and struggling for my own identity in my relationship with Ray, it was a major red flag that the relationship was not the right one for me. While it took me some time to act on that sign, I felt that something was off. When the relationship is right, it will not cost you your authentic self.

The challenge and gift that you face in an unfulfilling relationship may be speaking your truth, or it may be having the self-confidence to set standards and boundaries for your partner, or it may be having the courage to leave. There are a multitude of possibilities that might come up.

I know that there are sister friends who try very hard to attract love on a physical basis. You may be under the illusion that self-worth comes from appearance and how many people compliment and approach you. Unfortunately, when your self-worth is externally based, you will not find fulfillment through this route. It will continue to be a very frustrating and painful experience as you try to "compete" with younger women for men. You might trade sex for attention and love. It never works, and it is heartbreaking to observe women repeat this pattern throughout their lifetimes. Please do not let this be you.

Stand in the power that this radical decade brings you, knowing who you are and the richness of what you bring to any relationship. Remember to let that be the beacon for potential romantic partners to see and respond to. Here is the forty-something wisdom advantage that you embody that our twenty-something sisters have yet to grow into. We are not here simply for the pleasure of the "male gaze." Our worth is not created because men give their approval of our bodies. We do not deplete our divine energy or give ourselves away by showing our bodies indiscriminately. Of course, we enjoy feeling good, feeling sexy even, but our sense of self and sexiness have developed additional layers of depth so that we know not to throw our pearls before swine.

Know that you are valuable, and only those who recognize that get the keys to your kingdom. If you find yourself trying to attract a man with your T&A, here's a golden opportunity to do the spiritual work of self-reflection. Ask yourself: Why do I feel it necessary to dress or behave this way? Will I really be happy with the results it brings me? Has it ever really worked for me? If a man will follow my T&A, won't he follow the next woman's T&A too? What else can I value and cultivate in myself in addition to my body? What example do I need to set for others to follow in their treatment of me? What boundaries do I need to set?

Boundary Setting as a Sign of Self-Esteem

I had a university coworker who somehow regularly ended up working more hours than everyone else in support staff. I asked her one day, "Why are you still in the office on a holiday weekend when everyone has left early?" Her reply was, "Well, I was asked to stay and have everything in good shape for Tuesday when we get back." I simply stared at her in disbelief, and finally said, "You mean everyone else in your department left, and you feel responsible for making sure everything will run smoothly on Tuesday? Why?"

She said that she wanted to be viewed as a team player and flexible in responding to the needs of the department. I told her, "You know they only do that to you and no one else, and you know that is because you're the only one who says yes. Look around; no one else is here, and you really won't get any extra brownie points for this, because now everyone takes you for granted. Girl, get your stuff and get out of here! When they ask you on Tuesday, tell them you left for the weekend with everyone else."

I dragged her out with me, but she still felt bad about leaving. Her self-worth was determined by what other people thought of her. She felt that she had to earn people's appreciation by going the extra mile. She always felt so lucky to even have that job when everyone else seemed better qualified that she would never say no to any request. As we parted ways in the parking garage, I told her, "You deserve to have fun too. You deserve a break. Try to enjoy yourself." As long as I knew her, she never broke out of that mindset and habit. She never felt good enough, so she worked extra hard to prove herself. The problem was that she was her own harshest critic.

I certainly know the game of trading my authentic self for the approval, acceptance, or love of a man. Through my years of coaching and teaching, I know that it is helpful to hear someone else's story because we realize that we are not alone, not the only one who made that stupid choice or fell for that ridiculous story. We can forgive ourselves and move past shame and guilt. We can also begin to take that critical step back from the situation and gain enough perspective to learn the lessons, grow from the experience, and then engage life again on renewed terms. That's the key for the spiritual expansion of our souls. Don't just keep having the experience. Go within, find what's bruised inside yourself, connect the dots between all of your relationships that end up looking the same, and get an understanding about the ways in which your soul may be leading you.

Your higher self or angels, if you use that name, are helping you with these experiences, not torturing you. The number of painful relationship experiences you have are in direct proportion to how resistant you are to seeing your own patterns, the defense mechanisms that your ego has created, and the behaviors that result in you throwing your pearls before swine in an attempt to get someone else to love you when you don't love yourself. Dearest, your spiritual lessons will be repeated until learned, and there is no skipping a grade. It's best for your heart and soul that you plug in and get healed as soon as you can. That may have been hard to read, but listen, at forty-something it is time to be real and time to be clear. Do your self-examination, pay attention to your dominant belief systems, take ownership of all of your behaviors, and see the unfolding of the confident, clear, and courageous woman you can be. That's the transformation, and it's a beautiful thing if you will do the work.

Radical Lesson #8

Rely on Your Faith

Are you a person of faith? Even in the difficult, confusing times? Even when you've lost something or someone you felt you couldn't live without? When the person you thought you would marry left? When you lost your house? When your heart was broken because your dream seemed to fail?

My life had seemingly taken a turn for the worse, and I felt pretty near my wits' end. I was driving along in Los Angeles one day, near Brentwood, for those who might know, and my best friend, Rosemarie, was talking me down off the emotional cliff where I was pretty much living at that point. I figured I better pull over because I could feel a meltdown about to come over me. In recent months, I had painfully ended my four-year relationship, my business was losing traction despite my best efforts, I lost $6,500 in an internet phishing scam, my cat died, and I pretty much felt like a failure. I was depressed because I could not see how anything was going to get better anytime soon. Oh, and I had just bought a new car I had to pay for. I pulled over. I was silent. She found the words I needed: "I know it sucks, and honestly, I don't know why

---

40 Something Nugget of Wisdom

Faith in God, in your higher power or your higher self, in the spirits that guide you—that faith will get you through the pain and out the other side.

---

you are going through all of this at one time, but I do know that you will be okay. It will work out, and you will be okay. You always are. Just keep doing what you can, and you will be okay. Something will happen, and things will turn around—just like that. You can't see it now, but you know this. You teach other people this. You can't give up." Thank God for her in that moment. She was my lifeline during a very confusing, chaotic, scary time, and she reminded me that things do turn around.

Sometimes life really sucks! Sometimes you cannot see a light at the end of your tunnel. Sometimes these things happen all at once. I call this experience a divine reset from the universe in which everything we know gets called into question. We lose things—relationships, jobs, pets, people—and we are left wondering if we can recover. If we have faith, we can.

I hung on by faith. I prayed, meditated, and listened to spiritual teachings from people I admired. I reread books about how other people made it through difficult times. I put my affirmations on post-it notes around my bedroom. I reminded myself that I was simply being stretched and developing new muscles that I would need for the next stage of my evolution. I decided to see any and all opportunities that presented themselves as confirmation from God that, indeed, things were moving forward, and yes, I would be okay.

Listen to That Still, Small Voice

In my prayer time, I began to hear from that still, small voice a message that transformed everything: "It is time for some things to go. There is so much more for you if you are willing to release and trust." My dream world lit up with vivid, spiritual encounters, letting me know that I was on a path far beyond what meets the eye. I was reminded, "You are a spiritual being having a human experience, and all is well." I began to see the value in my difficult, crappy life experience. I concluded that it's not so crappy after all;

in fact, I'm still more privileged than most people on the planet. I was gaining a new level of emotional depth and compassion that I did not have previously. I realized that I had gained a new perspective about having things or knowing the right people. I grew. I began to truly know that *I am enough*, all by myself. The value of my life is not in what I have, where I live, what I drive, how much money I have, who I know, or what institutions I might or might not be affiliated with. I began to know, value, and trust myself, and it was real confidence, not dependent upon any external circumstance. My restoration began.

And with that deep-down authenticity that came from having to recreate myself, my world began to rebuild itself. I began to consciously observe that things that I had asked for were showing up in my life. For example, I would think, "Hmm, I need an extra $100 today," and lo and behold, $100 would show up somehow. Or, "I need to get a job for a while, I guess, but I still need my freedom," and then a good part-time gig fell into my lap. I remember thinking at one point, "Wait, did I just create that into my life? What else can I create if it's that easy?" Let me be clear: it's not that I'm any more magical than the next person. We all are magical creators. Sometimes when we are really feeling down, we turn to God or Spirit because there is no other option. There's no rich uncle or knight in shining armor coming. There's no magic wand. But we surrender and thereby allow God to show us tiny daily miracles.

Those tiny miracles shore us up in times of high anxiety and distress, and eventually they give us the confidence to step out again. In my case, I felt that I had nothing else to lose, so I had no reason not to try. I would think, "I have no idea what I'm doing or how it is going to turn out, but I'll at least show up." It was that little bit of willingness, that small step that I agreed to take, that created a new momentum. Previously closed doors began to open unexpectedly, influential people began to seek me out again, and the wheels were turning in my favor with very little effort on my part. Grace abounded in my life, and sometimes it moved me to tears, because clearly these were gifts and favors. I thought of the biblical story of Job (though my story was not that deep) and of his restoration after great loss of family, friends, fortune, and status. He came through it, and so would I. I just had to get out of my own way and trust the process, even though it felt like betrayal and loss because, yes, life is like that sometimes.

I won't tell you that you won't have periods of self-doubt and fear. Life experiences can be devastating. But I can truthfully tell you that it gets better. Get out of the way and allow it. Sometimes getting out of the way looks like forgiving someone or releasing anger. Sometimes it looks like saying, "I don't know, but I'm willing to try." Mostly, I think it looks like mustering up a mustard seed of faith and not giving up on yourself. That thought has allowed me to finally understand what my Grandma Jessie meant when she said, "It will be alright."

You might be scared, you might not know the answers, you might be broke, and you might feel as if you don't even trust your own judgment anymore, but you can trust that small voice within you that is nudging you toward the next stage of your evolution. Trust it implicitly, tell fear and doubt to have two seats, and do what the voice tells you to do. It is the very embodiment of God speaking to you. Instead of telling yourself that you don't know what to do, imagine that you do know, and that it is up to you to do it.

Sometimes guidance comes in the form of a bridge experience: when you receive a little grace, a gift, or an unexpected something that tides you over just when you need it most. It is that less-than-ideal job that comes up out of the blue when you have been unemployed for a year. It's that check in the mail that just covers the month's expenses. It is the person who shows up in your world at just the right moment, with just the right advice. A bridge experience is not an end in itself. It's a little carry-over that allows you to know that the universe is listening and responding. A bridge allows you to hold on a little longer. It is a respite in a grueling and stressful period of life. It carries you to the next stage, the next, longer bridge. You can trust it to take you as far as you need, until a new bridge presents itself, which will in turn take you to the next stage of your evolution.

Over time, in living this life, you will begin to recognize a bridge experience for what it is and joyfully walk along, knowing and trusting that all you need is provided, and so it continues. Some bridges are short, some are long, but they all serve the same purpose: to provide safe passage over troubled waters.

December 2014 and January 2015 were critical times when I thought that everything I had left came crashing down, and I was indeed scared to death. Then God came to get me, or so it seemed to me. What had happened to my life as I had known it, and what was I going to do next? These questions were constantly swirling in my head. Even when I seemed to be okay in the moment, my mind would say, "But what about the future? You have to figure something out and get back on track. You're losing ground every day. Do something!" It was completely crazy-making.

Then one day in February 2015, while picking up my takeout food order, I was given this download revelation from spirit and my higher self: "You had an appointed time of awakening in order to step into your real work, and so I came to get you, to remind you of it. It was not pleasant for you, as it meant the dissolution of your academic career as far as you could see, and along with it, the status and relative financial stability that you came to enjoy and expect as a college professor. But it was time for your awakening, so the rug was pulled away and the job was lost. Perfect! But then you did something tricky. Instead of focusing on yourself and stepping into your awakening, you allowed yourself to be swept into your boyfriend's life, and you remained there for nearly four years, during which time, you avoided yourself. Again, you were so caught up in the matrix of the 3-D world that I had to come for you again, to remind you, to awaken you. The Hollywood limelight was seductive and glamorous, and you jumped in eagerly to do what you usually do: give to others in exchange for them giving to you. That is an old paradigm for you, and it will no longer work, sorry! It did not work at the university in the way you had envisioned, and it would not work with Bill, no matter how much you tried."

Again, a revelation came into my world and rang the bell of awakening.

"Time to wake up! You are here for such a time as this! We have important work to do, contributing toward the spiritual expansion of humanity. A new type of human being is emerging, and you are part of the energetic shift that is participating in it, actually leading it. You have agreed to this work, and you called upon me to come in and use whatever means necessary to awaken you from your slumber. You were asleep at the wheel of your own life. You stayed in a relationship that you knew in your soul needed to end long before it did. Finally, you followed your guidance, and it dissolved too. All of your security seemed to come crashing down around you. Do you remember yet that you told me to do it? This is all by your design and agreement.

"If I get caught up in the three-dimensional matrix such that I am not about my work, come and get me. Disrupt anything else going on so that I awaken and get on with it."

And so I did. And so it is!

Theresa's Story

Theresa came to me as a client with several things on her plate, including a desire to become an entrepreneur as a speaker and author. Theresa had taken care of her terminally ill mother, who had recently passed away, and she was now beginning to think about how she would go about creating a new life of her own. Although she was in her forties, Theresa had not fully lived on her own much, never married or had children, and had never been able to pursue her dreams because she had spent most of her adult life after college living with and caring for her mother. Theresa admitted that she had no idea how to be a speaker, but that she felt excited about it and was ready to start putting pieces together, beyond her local Toastmasters speaking club.

The other challenge that Theresa faced was losing the house that she and her mother had shared. Theresa had mortgaged the house to pay for much of her mother's care over the years because insurance and Theresa's salary did not quite cover their expenses. She had been in the process of refinancing her home again when she hit several brick walls. She was unable to get approval, and she thought that foreclosure was imminent. I asked if she should even be hiring a coach at this time, but she believed she had to take the opportunity to turn her situation around and get guidance and support immediately. She told me that her mother had instilled a strong faith in God within her: "We always believed that God will show you a way when things look impossible, and I still believe that. There must be a way or I wouldn't have this dream or this gift."

Theresa had an amazingly rich speaking voice. She had often been recognized in her customer service jobs for her leadership style and charismatic bearing. She sounded like she should be on the stage as a performer, or at least on the radio. She had never done either, but she was eager to start somewhere if it would get her to her goal of professional speaking. I asked her to expand what this type of career might look like for her, and to brainstorm names of people she knew who might be connected to public platforms of any kind. She resisted, insisting she knew no one in those arenas.

After a week or so, I pushed her to think of any way she could get herself on her local radio station. She had a lightbulb revelation: "I do know someone! I have an old acquaintance I rarely see anymore, and she works in radio, but in another city. But I don't want to be that person calling from out of the blue asking for a job." I told her that she was going to be that person and she would see what came of it.

Feeling very awkward and embarrassed, she found a number for her friend and called. The friend was delighted to hear from her because she was soon relocating to Charlotte, North Carolina, where Theresa lived. She had heard through their network of friends about Theresa's mother's death and had wanted to reach out to her. To make a long story short, Theresa invited her friend to move in as a roommate who could help her pay the mortgage. Her friend also helped Theresa learn about broadcasting and radio.

This was a small breakthrough, but for Theresa it brought a much-needed bridge to her doorstep that enabled her to find her financial footing and even begin to step out toward her larger vision. When Theresa and I last spoke, she had worked something out with her bank with the help of advanced rent from her friend, and she was looking forward to hosting her new friends who worked in radio. She cried as she told me, "Now I know that my mother is watching out for me too. I have God and my mom, so I can't lose!"

Faith Will Lead You Through It

Often, our "luck" or opportunity hinges on a very ordinary or seemingly insignificant set of circumstances, like talking to an old friend. When we can see and act with an attitude of faith, having that sense that something has to give "if I just do my part," then we can move ourselves out of indifference or fear. When our starting point is faith, we seem to be able to hang on just a bit longer—until that bridge appears.

If you are familiar with the book of Esther in the Bible, you may recall that Esther is a young Jewish woman chosen to be queen under a foreign (non-Jewish) king. At the prodding of her older cousin, she concealed her true identity as a Jewish woman to get into the royal household. All was going well, until it wasn't. At a time of great persecution of the Jewish people, Esther stood to lose everything—her status, economic stability, possibly even her life—but she continued forward with the work she needed to do, starting with telling the truth and being authentic. She stood courageously at a time of great personal risk and made her claim for her people and herself. I use this story as a way of illustrating that sometimes we think we have it all, only to see it threatened or, indeed, stripped away. Can you recognize that something bigger and greater might be trying to unfold through you, and that you simply need to be willing to trust yourself and be yourself? What do you have in those moments to carry you through in the face of your fear?

Radical Lesson #9

Take Time for Self-Care

You've heard this a million times in some form or fashion: "You have to teach people how to treat you." Let's consider this a little more deeply. What does it signify that we would allow ourselves to work to exhaustion and set aside self-care? Do we think that we are going to get extra brownie points in heaven for working extra hard? Is it the American Protestant work ethic that teaches us that hard work and godliness are connected? Is it a voice in our own minds admonishing us not to be lazy slackers? (That one gets me.) Whatever it is for you, there is a dominant story that shapes us into thinking that we have to work to exhaustion, always be "on," and be super busy with all of our electronic devices nearly 24/7. For many people, being busy gives them a feeling of legitimacy, an identity, and a sense of importance.

And to that end, we neglect ourselves. We don't seem to find it useful or valuable to be busy focusing on ourselves, nurturing our own souls, or listening to our own inner callings. All of our busyness is outwardly focused—how many emails we need to send, how many meetings we have to attend, how little time we have to

---

40 Something Nugget of Wisdom

Whatever self-care looks like for you, the most important thing is to remember to breathe and take it easy. Trust, allow, be in the flow of life. All is well.

---

cultivate relationships. That's why we think of self-care as an afterthought. We think of it as being selfish, pampered, or spoiled. We would all do better to rethink that old phrase, "Give until it hurts." It is not wise to give from a depleted state.

Let your new forty-something perspective, life experience, and well-earned wisdom be the catalyst to not just do better, but to know better through seasoned discernment about how you will spend your precious life energy. Don't just go along to get along anymore. This includes respecting any teaching that says you should ignore your own well-being in the quest for riches, fame, self-worth, or someone else's expectations. What could be more important than taking care of yourself? What do you have to give if you have nothing?

Doing It for Yourself

I'm an advocate for us to fall in love with taking care of ourselves. I can tell you from my own experience and the experiences shared with me from other women over the years that selfless over-giving leads you directly into the brick wall of resentment, anger, and bitterness—no exceptions! We are meant to have rest, to take a Sabbath, to sit and contemplate, and to hear our own inner guidance. Take peace and solace knowing that doing "nothing" can really be doing the most important something. Chasing things or "hustling for your self-worth" won't lead you anywhere you want to go.

At forty-something, you can give yourself permission to take care of yourself. If you can't get approval from anyone else, give it to yourself because you know, value, and trust yourself. That includes listening to your body when it tells you to slow down, take a nap, stretch, or eat this, not that. Listen to your spirit when it tells you to turn off your phone and sit in silence for a while. Learn to be comfortable with silence; listen to your own heartbeat. Set up rituals for yourself that are meaningful. They don't have to be complicated.

Here is a simple one that I created for myself. I have loved to read since I first learned how. Over the years I have always valued reading and collecting books. However, somehow I let other things push that great love to the wayside, though my spirit longed for it regularly. In recent years, at forty-something, I established "reading hour" for myself. I decided that I would create a routine, a tradition for myself, and reading hour was born: I committed to reserve at least three hours per week for pleasure reading. If one planned day does not work, I do not let it slide; I move it to the next day. It's a non-negotiable, self-honoring ritual integrated into my regular life. I don't have to wait for the perfect time, save up money, or travel someplace special to do it. I just decide that it is important to me, and I honor it. Can you do that for yourself with something that is meaningful to you?

Ladies, what about your appearance and sense of well-being? Forty-something really is fabulous these days. We have many resources available to us that help us stay looking healthy and beautiful. Of course, you have to honor yourself enough to use them. What have you let go? Where are you cheating yourself out of self-loving care that you deserve and desire? How many times have you made an appointment for that manicure, massage, or facial only to cancel it because something came up? Have you ever started saving money for a vacation or something else you really wanted, only to raid your savings to bail someone else out of trouble?

What do your hair and skin look like? Your teeth? Your body? You are a reflection of your own care. Are you looking your best as you live and thrive in your forties? Do you avoid looking at yourself? Can you own your own beauty and nurture it to your own liking? It's not about trying to look like someone else or fit a beauty standard other than your own. After all, this decade gives us the confidence to decide for ourselves what we want to look like. I'm advocating for you to simply like how you look and feel, or else value yourself enough to make the changes you want to see.

If someone gives you a compliment, do you deflect it or receive it? Maybe you are in a professional environment where you have found it necessary or just easier to "tone down" your appearance. Are you in a "boys' club" profession, where your existence there is already suspect, and so you minimize your natural beauty to fit in and be taken more seriously? How does it feel to do this to yourself? Although it may have become "normal" because you've done it for years, how does it affect the spirit of who you are? It is difficult to stand in authentic alignment if you are turning down your light in any circumstance. If you find yourself in such an environment, how would it be for you to go to work dressed as yourself or wearing your hair the way you really want to?

Don't Take Your Health for Granted

Exhaustion does not have to be your teacher! Let's talk about our health and well-being. More women than ever before are suffering heart attacks. More women are dying by suicide. We know that women's health has somehow become a political quagmire as male politicians argue over what a woman may or may not do with her own body. All of that aside, you must care for your own body, mind, and soul. If you are like most women, you have made every effort to be superwoman, or due to circumstance, you have had to work exceedingly hard to survive. In any case, your body has shown you that with neglect comes pain, discomfort, and dis-ease.

In my case, I have been on a superwoman mission, hustling for my self-worth. In my thirties I nearly collapsed on a couple of different occasions in my effort to do everything and do it perfectly. The first time that I recall happened while I was working on my master's degree in theology. I was attending seminary just outside of Columbus, Ohio. I had been juggling work and school, and pretty much ignoring my body's signs to slow down. I began having long, heavy, and irregular periods. I would bleed for two weeks at a time sometimes and find myself dizzy and extremely tired. Nevertheless, I continued my hectic pace of checking off everything on my "have to do" list, until the day I almost fainted and fell off a stool in the school library as I reached up to grab a book from a high shelf. On that day I decided that I should go to the doctor and find out what all this bleeding was about.

I learned that I had uterine fibroids, benign masses of tissue that form in and around the uterus. These are exceptionally common in African American women and often lead to a hysterectomy. My mother and aunt had also had them. In my case, I had a dilation and curettage (D&C) procedure that worked for me, at least for a while. I also learned that I had to slow down. I had no energy due to persistent blood loss resulting in anemia, so I had to rest more, eat well, take iron supplements, and just take a time out. Of course, this slowdown caused me to have additional anxiety about everything that I was not getting done. I tried to force my recovery at one point, only to find myself in a bathroom stall, again while at school, having a full-on, hyperventilating, racing-heart, head-swimming anxiety attack.

Over the years following that episode, I had two more fibroid events that eventually led me to have surgery and a follow-up embolization procedure. I share this rather detailed story because I have met many women who also suffer from fibroids but won't stop long enough to care for themselves. As I mentioned, it is extremely common: some sources report that one in three African American women will have them. I can personally attest that most black women I know currently have fibroids or have had a bout with fibroids in the past. I have had conversations with women in hair salons, restaurant bathrooms, social gatherings, and airports wherein we share stories and nightmare episodes about embarrassing bleeding that sapped the joy right out of our lives. Even so, many women I've spoken to have not gotten treatment. They remain afraid that they will have to have a hysterectomy and won't be able to have children. Or they are simply afraid of any surgical procedure. Fear overtakes their good sense, and they continue dragging themselves through their days feeling worn-out and anxious.

Did I mention how this condition can also severely compromise your sex life? Heavy bleeding for twelve or more days a month makes it hard to have sex comfortably. Oh, and even if you are not bleeding at that moment, the act of sex can bring it on again. Some women begin to avoid regular social activities for fear of having an accident at any given time. Some women constantly carry a stash of tampons, pads, panties, and extra clothes because they don't know what might happen. And they can never wear white! All of this begins to erode a woman's sense of fun, enthusiasm, and spontaneity.

Maybe you are familiar with the biblical story of the woman with an issue of blood (Mark 5:25). The woman has bled for twelve years and spent all she has trying to be cured. Twelve years! Then she hears that Jesus will be passing by, and she becomes determined to see him and be healed. In the story she manages to touch the hem of his garment and get her healing. Having myself been a woman with an issue of blood, I will forever read her story with much compassion.

You Don't Have to Be Superwoman

That lesson should have been enough, but then in 2012, I must have had my superwoman cloak on again. I was just leaving one of my survival jobs, and I was bone-tired. I had been burning the candle at both ends for a year, and I was frazzled and exhausted. All I could think about was, How can I escape? How can I get away? I wanted to quit working so hard, but fear kept saying, "But what will you do? You know how it feels to be broke. Now that you have a little, you better keep at these jobs. Take every opportunity you can. What if you end up with nothing?" This is the tape that played in my head as I was driving home. Then I received the intuitive download: "Life does not have to be like this. You are creating it this way, and you can stop this anytime you want. Have faith that all is provided. No one asks that you work yourself to the bone for your survival, but it is your belief system that keeps all this in place as necessary. What do you really want to do? Like really, for yourself?"

I was afraid of my answer, because of course I knew that it would mean something scary and unknown. Quit that job! Trust that the next step would be provided. Fear loomed large, yet I was hearing the call of my higher self, my inner knowing that said, "Come this way." It's not that anything was wrong with my job, but it had served its purpose in my life as a bridge, and now it was time to move on. My own higher version of myself was telling me, "Remember who you are. Time to move on." And yet I deliberated, feeling obligated to my employers and coworkers, whom I felt I couldn't abandon. We were all just starting to gel together, even though the job was demanding.

I knew in that instant that working like that was a projection of my belief system that tells me that I must Be Responsible and Work Really Hard! But now I could consciously see it, and I was able to look at it from afar, and say, "Nope, no more of this. I'm going to trust my instinct that says it is time for me to move on, and that the next stage, step, bridge, or path will open up." This was a transformational moment for my whole life. It set the stage for a new, empowered belief system that says, "I really can trust myself and follow my own path."

That moment changed everything for me. That's when I really began to take the S off of my chest; I let superwoman take a seat and put her feet up.

Part of my lesson in that scenario was that I realized that I felt obligated to do what others wanted me to do, to perform, to do well, to make others happy and comfortable. It was all my mother wanted: for me to work hard and do well. *No excuses.* I couldn't let her down. I simply could not fail or disappoint her. Even though she'd died over twenty-five years ago, her voice still rang in my head loud and clear!

But the truth is that bar was unnaturally high, excessive, and burdensome. I was fortunate that I had not had some kind of physical or emotional breakdown. No amount of hearing otherwise from spiritual teachers, gurus, or the like could counteract my mental tape before I learned to trust instinct. Exhaustion had indeed become my teacher because I created my own lesson that way. It is as if I had to find out for myself that this was not the way. A more enlightened, more conscious way of living is to value *being*, not just *doing*. I had to show myself that over-working and over-giving will not get me extra brownie points, and it is not required.

I share my experience here because, if this is you too, I want you to know that you can be healed. Release your fear of the What If monster, and be empowered and courageous enough to value your life. It is your divine right to have an abundant, joyous, healthy life. Take care of yourself.

Where to Start

If you don't even know where to start, start here: as an act of self-love I encourage the mirror exercise. Stand in front of a mirror completely naked and look at yourself. Now name three to five things that you like—more if you can. As women we tend to be very self-critical, in constant comparison mode, and unable to acknowledge our beauty and value. In your forties you can give yourself permission to love yourself, and if you decide to change something, it is your empowered choice.

You can also give yourself permission to say no when other people's requests and demands have become too much for you. Saying no is sometimes necessary for your own well-being. Protecting your own time and energy is a radical act of self-care, and it doesn't cost a thing! Turn your phone off for a set time every day. We're old enough to know how to live without it, right? I have found that even the notification pings from social media and text messages add to my stress level. Turning off the sound entirely gives me back a little mental peace.

Treat yourself to the value and healing effect of silence. Recover quiet time, even if it is just within your own bathroom. Remember the library? Go there for the quiet. An interesting sign of our times is the amount of time most of us spend in our cars. You can reclaim this space, and turn it into your own personal meditation temple. I know of many working women who take to their cars at some point during their day to breathe, read scripture, journal, meditate, or even sleep. Mothers of young children tell me that they value this time because no one is looking for them or expecting anything from them for these thirty to sixty minutes. Even if you are not able to do it every day, you can make a deal with yourself to reclaim car time a couple of days a week. In some workplaces, there are wellness options for employees. Check out what might be available to you at low or no cost.

Your well-being is ultimately up to you. Will you prioritize yourself? The world will continue to spin on its axis, and deadlines will always loom. Will you be there for yourself?

Radical Lesson #10

Remember That You Are Enough

There comes a point, at least potentially, when we realize that we are good enough just as we are. There comes a point in the realm of experiences and maturity where we simply stop asking for permission or seeking outside validation for our choices or our being.

Stop Hustling for Worthiness

Brené Brown, a college professor, social worker, and now bestselling author, talks in her 2010 presentation, *The Hustle for Worthiness: Exploring the Power of Love, Belonging, and Being Enough*, about how people, often women, "hustle for worthiness." I like that term because it gives a clear visual about how we go into performance mode when we are feeling inadequate. We become willing to exchange ourselves for some semblance of attention from another. The outside gaze or touch signals to us that we are worthy, lovable, enough, accepted, good, smart, and desirable. For many of us, that external gaze is the only signal we recognize. Our internal barometer is broken and untrustworthy. Herein lies the problem.

Worthiness is an inside job, and it requires a working barometer as true and trusted as our very own breath. No amount of people

---

40 Something Nugget of Wisdom
Worthiness is an inside job, and it requires a working barometer as true and trusted as our very own breath.

---

pleasing to extract praise from another will be sufficient. No number of sexual partners will fill the void. No amount of sexualized attention in bars, on the street, or on social media will make you feel good about yourself if you don't already feel good about yourself. In fact, their presence and the inevitable emotional or physical absence will only cause you to feel worse and even less worthy, because every time you seek attention, you are giving a little piece of yourself to someone or something that can't possibly give you what you really need. It's a losing hustle, and a game in which women in particular lose miserably.

What's really lacking is one's self. There is a spiritual void in this game: a lack of self-knowledge, self-value, self-worth, and an overall lack of meaning. It can turn our own self-protective ego into a thirsty beast who, in turn, causes us to perform our way into a fragmented and temporary sense of worthiness. What Brené Brown calls "hustle for worthiness" I call throwing your pearls before swine. By either name, this behavior will likely end with you picking up the pieces of your devastated heart at the end of it all.

There must be consistency and alignment within you, and in relationship between you and your outer world. There is a great but sometimes subtle disturbance internally when we betray ourselves in any way, great or small. Anytime we override our own intuition, body wisdom, still small voice, or however you may describe it, we experience dis-ease.

I have noticed that, throughout the forties decade, small issues we have been living with for a long time become too much to bear. It is as if our own spirit says, *"Enough! I must be myself, and I don't care what other people think!"* I love this moment in the lives of women because it is a spark of self-awakening. It can be a difficult moment when you are living through it, because there may be pushback from others who are not used to you living in your power.

However, it has the potential to be a breakthrough moment, calling you back to yourself. I'm all for that!

As much as we say that we want change in our lives at any given point, when that change actually happens, many of us are scared to death, terrified into paralysis, and eager to run for cover and comfort. We try to shrink back into our comfort zones, though we were just previously lamenting that zone as boring, stagnant, and limited. I learned to trust myself to the extent that fear no longer stops me. I've gotten comfortable with uncertainty. I don't have to have all the answers. I trust that the outcome will be what I need ultimately. How did this come about?

It came about through losing many of the external things that I thought I needed to be safe and secure. When I lost my university job, I felt that I lost a part of my status and identity. That required finding a new identity not based on external employment or affiliation. When my relationship broke down, I lost another sense of security and borrowed identity. I had to find myself within myself, and reclaim my truest self. When my business suffered, and money was scarce, I had to pick up other work that I never thought I would have to do again. But when bills have to be paid, I learned to hustle and work where I could work for a while. It taught me self-reliance, resilience, and renewed persistence.

I also learned what my faith was really about. I prayed constantly. I spoke to my angels, guides, and higher self all day, every day. I immersed myself in scriptures and meditation. I knew that faith would see me through, and each day I looked for signs that circumstances were again turning my way.

Through these experiences I learned to appreciate myself and to be proud of myself. I still struggle with workaholism as a symptom of trying to prove myself, but now I bring another perspective that reminds me that I am enough. I will not be killing myself softly while pretending that everything is okay. I will tell my truth, and I will roll with the punches, however that goes.

I began to internalize the idea of being enough the hard way: through sheer exhaustion from trying too hard, over-giving, and trying to prove myself. Crashed out on my sofa one Friday night, mindlessly watching TV (probably shopping channels) to rest my overtaxed nerves, I began questioning myself, Who is all of this for? Why is this my favorite thing to do on a Friday night? And then came my most enlightened thought, one that has truly saved me from myself ever since: What if this (meaning my life) was as good as it gets? Could I be happy with myself, or do I imagine myself in my senior years regretting that I somehow fell short of some goal? Would I still be beating myself up for not achieving some next-level accolade? Would I really consider myself a failure if I did not grasp that next golden ring? Well, as I thought about it like that, so much came into perspective. Of course I would not be a failure at life! What is this insane measuring stick that I hold myself to, and who is measuring me?

That was an emotional moment for me because I realized that I was a harsh judge and critic of myself, and that I had been holding myself back from enjoying my life more because I was so busy working my fingers to the bone. I declared enough already! I declared that I am enough already, and that any additional accomplishments from that time forward would be icing on my cake. I've already "proven myself" to the memory of my mother. Since that time, I've found the grace that allows me to enjoy my life that much more. I appreciate that I did not have to struggle and climb my way to the top of something, and I can just exhale, be myself, and do the things that I enjoy doing just for fun.

Find Your Way to Self-Acceptance

Women who find their way to me often suffer from this disorder too. In my personal journal I labeled it *Burnt-Out Overachieving Perfectionist Syndrome.* Can you relate? Unfortunately, we usually come to ourselves through some sort of crisis. I've seen women struggle with a crisis in their health, mental wellness, finances, or relationships, and then come to the life-giving revelation that the root cause is some form of overachieving or perfectionism that has been driving them to their wits' end, a therapist's couch, a hospital bed, or anxiety-ridden sessions with me as they try to figure out what happened to their carefully cultivated lives.

By this time, a woman's coping mechanisms are failing. She is not able or willing to continue pushing herself to absurd lengths. Of course, she is usually criticizing herself harshly and feeling like a failure despite her obvious successes and achievements in life to date. Our work dives right into the root cause of the disorder, that sense of *not* being enough that propels us into *over*doing, just to feel okay. Her resume may be stellar, she may have awards and public recognition all around her, she may have a beautiful home, and yet . . . there are those other things over there somewhere on her colleague's resume or in her neighbor's house that she must have too. Then she will measure up and finally be Good Enough.

It's vicious, because there is no end to this exhausting cycle, and what's more is that she gets praise and compliments for it all along the way. "See, Mom? I'm doing okay, right?" And depending on Mom's answer, real or imagined, she gets up the next day and returns to the grindstone, sometimes eagerly, until the moment when she's home on a Friday night in jammies hoping the phone never rings again.

This syndrome is a chronic condition, but it can be managed, and you can have peace of mind, joy, and contentment in your life. Self-acceptance is my prescription. You can treat yourself with doses of grace and self-care. Reward yourself with quiet time, activities you enjoy that have nothing to do with work, and little things that maybe you have forgotten that you like. I took up art journaling! I didn't even know that this was a thing, but when I discovered it, I bought a bunch of journals and art pads. Instead of using them for writing, I use them for watercolor and collaging. Again, who knew? I never thought of myself as having artistic talent, but it doesn't matter—it's fun.

There simply came a point when I decided to let myself off the hook. I attribute this epiphany not only to exhaustion but to my spiritual practice as well. As I made more room for my meditation and other practices to expand, I was reminded that all is well. Life is not supposed to be rough-and-tumble, and dog-eat-dog. My spirituality reminded me about nurturance, ease, and grace. I was reminded to observe nature, and in particular my cat Chloe, who somehow manages to get all of her needs met without much effort at all. She sleeps a lot, stretches, grooms, purrs, runs around frenetically for a fraction of her day, and then goes back to stretch and lie down again. Nature is a good teacher for peace and recharging. Many indigenous religious practices revolve around the cycles and wisdom of nature. We do well to revisit some of these teachings. Resistance is a struggle; moving with the current is easy and life-giving.

When there is a disruption in nature, the animals shake it off and rebalance. I think as humans we sometimes forget the rebalancing part, but as my Grandma Jessie would say, "You're gonna get this lesson, one way or another." Here you are at forty-something. Are you getting your lesson?

Conclusion

My forties have taught me to walk my talk on faith, perseverance, self-confidence, self-nurturance, and following my bliss, or as I now think of it, creating the life I want to live on my own terms, with full confidence that it will be so. Most of us have no idea about our inherent power. Many of us come from religious upbringings in which we were not taught that we could directly connect to the God of our understanding or that a benevolent higher power is available to help us create our lives in meaningful ways. I am here to remind you that you are deserving, and that you can create the life you want to live.

Prior to my forties, I struggled with questions of authentic identity, my life's purpose, and determining what I really wanted rather than just doing what others expected of me. Many other women go through a similar struggle. At a certain point, you must know it, declare it, own it, and walk in it; otherwise you will die unfulfilled and even resentful and angry because you gave too much and no one appreciated you. Your needs went unmet because you could not articulate what you wanted and needed. You felt you had no personal power. But the truth is that you do have power. And you can learn to embrace and use it.

Many of us on a certain spiritual path believe that we are creating our own realities, yet we struggle with manifesting the thing or situation we most want. We seek answers from external authorities, gurus, books, affirmations, or meditation practices, and still feel that we can't quite get to where we want to be. The gift that I have discovered about manifesting—that is, bringing your desires into fruition—is that it gets easier when you are clear in purpose, confident in your being, and authentic in your alignment with your desired outcome. What doesn't work is pleading or being in a state of fear, trying to bring about the love of your life or a new job opportunity out of desperation. What does work is acknowledging your own personal power, which you can develop.

Remember: don't accept your limitations, let go of resistance, believe it can be so, and allow it to flow into your experience without effort or strain. Know that you are creating your circumstances, and that you can create a life you love. And because you have the additional wisdom of being forty-something, you know that you can weather any storm, flow with life's changes, and still be okay. So if all does not go exactly as planned, regroup and try again. The gift of confidence is everything. It opens many doors and slays many dragons that used to keep you stuck. It allows you to feel comfortable in your own skin, and finally take ownership of your own life.

What's the key to manifesting anything you want? Say it with me, "I can create anything I want, and today I want . . ." Now go wash the dishes or have a cocktail, and forget about how it will happen. Trust in the restoration.

While it's true that not every ounce of self-doubt fades away in the forties, I love that we have enough confidence, clarity, and courage to make authentic choices. The forties decade is a season unto itself. It is a decade beautifully and precisely preparing us for an entirely new level of expansiveness and freedom in our fifties.

Afterword

It has literally taken every day (and then some) of my forties to write and complete this book. Now that I am in fact fifty-one, I understand why. I've grown throughout the decade, but particularly between forty-eight and fifty, I've had the experiences and the heightened insight to be able to glean wisdom from them in expanded ways. I look at the picture of myself at my fortieth birthday party, and think, "You had no idea what life lessons you were in for!"

The relationship I had after I ended the one with Bill lasted two years. Again, I learned tremendous amounts about myself. It seems that as soon as I reached the end of my forty-ninth year, I was hit with a major revelation. This spiritual download came upon me like a lightning bolt from my beloved angel, who once again reminded me of something so true that I was riveted by its simplicity and its profundity all at once. She said, "Your main relationship challenge in this lifetime has been to learn how to love without losing yourself." Wow! This little piece of wisdom rang through my entire system as if I had never heard these words before. I mean, I teach these things! I recognize this when I see it in other people. But I did not ever see how strongly it was playing out in my own life.

I realized that the fear of losing myself in a relationship caused me to avoid marriage and deep commitment. My most recent relationships have been about this, with me literally arguing and struggling with my partners for my true self and voice. It is *exceptionally* clear to me now how I attracted that. I involved myself in relationships that would require me to establish and maintain my own boundaries. It is indeed possible to have intimate relationships and still maintain my own identity, vision, and voice. Of course, this new perspective changes everything, including the new partners I now attract. As the life lesson is learned, I no longer have to fight that battle inside or out.

It is the same for you. As you learn your lessons, you will find that you no longer have to fight those same old battles anymore. Your life becomes smoother in these once-complicated and painful areas. You graduate from that class. Rest assured there are more lessons for you, but as you get more lessons under your belt, your confidence increases, and you do not feel overwhelmed or hopeless. You know for sure that this too shall pass, and you will be okay. That is worth everything!

How are you navigating your forties? If you recognize yourself here in these pages, and would like support on your personal journey, write me and let me know how I can help you: drdarnise@drdarnisemartin.com.

Acknowledgments

I would like to give special thanks to a few people who have been an important part of my journey and those who have helped me to finally give birth to this project.

First, I have to thank my Thornton-Martin family for always giving me that supportive push to set big goals and accomplish them! Indeed, it takes a village.

Second, to my circle of friends who have encouraged me through this process for years. Thanks for your patience and ongoing support as I talked through all of my ideas.

Last, my editor/project manager/midwife, Beth Wright, for her help at multiple stages of finally pushing this baby out. "I just want to be finished, Beth."

Thank you for reading my book!

I would appreciate your feedback so that I can make the next version of this book even better and plan future books. Please leave me an honest review on Amazon, letting me know what you thought of *40 Something*. Thanks so much!

—Dr. Darnise

www.ingramcontent.com/pod-product-compliance
Lightning Source LLC
Chambersburg PA
CBHW060304010526
44108CB00042B/2668